KIDNAPPED BY HEZBOLLAH
Freed by Purpose

KIDNAPPED BY HEZBOLLAH

Freed by Purpose

Dr. Kaushik Sridhar

Published by Brolga Publishing Pty Ltd
ABN 46 063 962 443
PO Box 452
Torquay 3228 VIC
Australia

email: markzocchi@brolgapublishing.com.au

All rights reserved. No part of this publication may be reproduced, stored in a retrieval system or transmitted in any form or by any means electronic, mechanical, photocopying, recording or otherwise without prior permission from the publisher.

Copyright © Kaushik Sridhar 2025
ISBN: 9781-7636-801-80

Printed in Australia
Cover design by Luke Harris, WorkingType Studio
Typeset by WorkingType Studio

BE PUBLISHED

Publish through a successful publisher.
Brolga Publishing is represented through:
• National book trade distribution, including sales, marketing & distribution through Simon & Schuster.
• International book trade distribution to:
    - The United Kingdom
    - Sales representation in South East Asia
• Worldwide e-Book distribution

For details and enquiries, contact:
Brolga Publishing Pty Ltd
ABN 46 063 962 443
PO Box 452
Torquay Victoria 3228
Australia

markzocchi@brolgapublishing.com.au
(Email for a catalogue request)

This book is, at its heart, a journey across borders, through purpose, and into self. And no journey is ever truly complete without a companion who brings laughter to the detours, grace to the chaos, and meaning to the miles.

To my wife – my partner in every sense: thank you for walking beside me, not just through airports and alleyways, but through every moment of growth and reflection. Your courage, curiosity, and deep sense of purpose inspire me daily. You have always been more than a travel partner – you've been my compass.

To those who've shared stories, offered shelter, asked difficult questions, or simply listened: your presence helped shape this narrative.

And to the reader: may you find the courage to step into the unknown, the wisdom to pause when it matters, and the joy of discovering something new – within the world, and within yourself.

CONTENTS

Prologue	the Search for Meaning	1
Part 1	**The Beauty of Travel**	**5**
Chapter 1	The Transformative Power of Travel	7
Chapter 2	The Early Years: Lessons from Nigeria and India	12
Chapter 3	The Complexities of Identity: America and Australia	17
Chapter 4	The Middle East: A Journey That Changed Everything	22
Chapter 5	The Beauty of Humanity and the Reality of Danger	28
Chapter 6	Travel as a Path to Self-Discovery	33
Part 2	**The Middle Eastern Adventure**	**39**
Chapter 7	Apprehension and Excitement: Planning the Journey	41
Chapter 8	The Journey Begins — Melbourne to Lebanon via Qatar	45
Chapter 9	Discovering Lebanon: Beauty, History, and Sorrow	49
Chapter 10	The Generosity of Strangers — Kindness in the Heart of Lebanon	55
Chapter 11	Dahiyeh: The Start of the Hezbollah Adventure	59
Chapter 12	The Hezbollah Encounter — Kidnapped in Dahiyeh	61
Chapter 13	My Reflection	83
Chapter 14	Journey into Syria: A Land of Contrasts	88
Chapter 15	The Journey into Iraq — From Chaos to Kindness	94
Chapter 16	Iraqi Kurdistan: Connection Amidst Tranquility	98
Chapter 17	After the Trip: Changed Perspectives	100

Part 3	**The Professional Pivot**	**103**
Chapter 18	The Corporate World: Success and Stagnation	104
Chapter 19	Confronting the Question of Purpose	108
Chapter 20	The Leap of Faith	111
Part 4	**Finding Meaning in Life's Journey**	**121**
Chapter 21	The Intersection of Travel and Purpose	122
Chapter 22	Resilience, Impact, and Looking Forward	141
Conclusion	A Journey to Authentic Purpose	147
Chapter 23	The Power of Perspective	148
Chapter 24	From Stagnation to Freedom	153
Chapter 25	Purpose Beyond Profit	160
Chapter 26	The Practice of Resilience	165
Chapter 27	A Life of Purpose	171

Prologue

THE SEARCH FOR MEANING

Looking back, it's hard to pinpoint the exact moment I began searching for purpose. Maybe it was during a restless night in early 2020, the world around me transformed by the pandemic, my career suddenly uncertain. Perhaps it was when I watched my father struggle for life in ICU, or when I found myself questioning the corporate ladder I'd climbed for years. Or maybe it was a far deeper itch, one that had been quietly gnawing at me—a longing to find meaning beyond titles, pay cheques, and societal expectations.

When the pandemic hit, it was as if the universe pressed pause on life as I knew it. In the span of a few months, I lost my job, and my father's health wavered on the brink. The world I had known—structured, secure, full of predictable routines—became unrecognisable. Faced with an uncertain future, I found myself wrestling with questions I had been able to ignore for years: What am I truly here to do? What does success mean when stripped of career accomplishments? And is there a way to create a lasting impact that transcends titles and job roles?

These questions lingered like shadows, especially as I navigated the chaotic job market and struggled to find a way forward. I eventually did secure a new role, which I took with gratitude but quickly realised wasn't the solution to the deeper questions. I had thought that simply being employed again would restore my sense of direction, but instead, it revealed the fragility of my attachment to the corporate world. I began to wonder if there was more, something that couldn't be measured in quarterly reports or bonuses.

For years, I'd worked my way through the corporate maze, moving up in roles and responsibilities, collecting accolades, awards, and endorsements. But there was always something missing. In quiet moments, I often thought of the concept of "purpose," a word so frequently tossed around in meetings, mission statements, and networking events. Purpose and impact became corporate buzzwords, things everyone claimed to understand. Yet, as I encountered more people and climbed higher, I realised few truly understood what those words meant. To them, purpose was little more than a set of KPIs, and impact was often reduced to metrics on a spreadsheet.

But deep down, I knew it was more than that. Over the years, I'd faced enough adversity—both professionally and personally—that I knew purpose couldn't be quantified so neatly. I'd experienced the kind of hardship that shapes a person. As a child, I had faced bullying, an outsider in a foreign country, desperate to prove my worth. I'd endured racial slights in the workplace, moments that tested my confidence and resolve. Later, I'd face challenges with my wife—a lifelong journey of resilience, love, and mutual support.

And then there were the close brushes with death. Twice, I had come face-to-face with my own mortality, each time feeling the unsettling rush of fear followed by an eerie calm. I'd nearly died in a plane crash. I'd even had a gun pressed against my head once. Each of these experiences left a mark, a scar on the soul, and a lingering reminder that life is fragile. Life can change in an instant, and I could lose everything in a heartbeat.

By the time 2023 rolled around, I was desperate for a change. My wife and I planned a trip to the Middle East—a journey that would, as I would later realise, redefine my understanding of purpose and resilience. Initially, she was reluctant, her concerns underscored by the media's portrayal of the region as fraught with risk. And I understood her apprehension; travelling through Syria, Iraq, Lebanon, and the Kurdish regions wasn't a conventional holiday. But something within me yearned to go, to experience this region firsthand, and she ultimately agreed, saying it would be the trip of a lifetime. And she was right.

Arriving in the Middle East, I found a world that defied my expectations. It was a region brimming with history, beauty, and resilience, despite the scars of conflict. In Lebanon, I found myself in awe of people who had endured years of political unrest and economic hardship, yet were still generous and warm. In Syria, I met families living amidst the rubble of war-torn cities, their spirits undiminished, their eyes filled with a quiet strength. In Iraq, I was touched by the resilience of communities rebuilding lives in the shadows of violence and loss.

These encounters were humbling. The people I met lived with a purpose I had seldom seen—a purpose rooted not in accomplishments or ambition but in survival, community, and hope. They showed me that resilience isn't about pretending hardships don't exist; it's about rising each day despite them. They lived with a kind of courage that I had only glimpsed in my life before, a courage born not of choice but of necessity.

As we travelled through these regions, I began to see purpose as something more than a personal quest for fulfilment. Purpose was about connection, empathy, and the impact we have on others, even if in small, quiet ways. Purpose, I realised, is about facing life with authenticity, embracing both the beauty and the hardship. It is about creating ripples of kindness, leaving people better than you found them, and learning from every encounter, no matter how brief.

This book is my attempt to document this journey—not just across foreign lands but across the landscapes of the mind and soul. It is a journey through fear, resilience, love, and transformation. It is a reflection on the people who left their mark on me and a tribute to those who live with purpose despite life's challenges.

I hope that as you read, you find pieces of your own story within these pages. Perhaps you, too, have questioned your purpose, wrestled with adversity, or faced moments that left you changed forever. My journey may be unique, but the search for meaning is universal. And if there's one thing I've learned, it's this: true purpose is found not in achievements but in the courage to live honestly, the grace to lift others, and the strength to keep going, no matter what.

This journey isn't about discovering purpose once and for all; it's about choosing purpose every day, in small and large ways. I invite you to join me on this journey, and perhaps, along the way, you'll find a piece of your own purpose, too.

Part 1
THE BEAUTY OF TRAVEL

Chapter 1

THE TRANSFORMATIVE POWER OF TRAVEL

Travel has always been more than just a hobby for me—it's been a lifeline, a compass guiding me through the complexities of life. Growing up across different continents, from India to Nigeria, the United States to Australia, travel became an intrinsic part of my identity. It wasn't just about moving from one place to another; it was about shifting perspectives, expanding my worldview, and understanding that the world is far larger, more complex, and more beautiful than we can imagine when standing still. Travel, I've found, has a way of revealing what lies beneath the surface—not just of other cultures, but also of our own hearts and minds.

In each place I lived or visited, I found not only new environments but new ways of understanding life itself. Travel became a mirror, reflecting back aspects of myself I hadn't yet seen, and a lens through which I could examine my values, priorities, and purpose. From an early age, I realised that travelling wasn't just about destinations—it was about journeying within. And every new place I visited seemed to bring me closer to understanding who I was and who I wanted to be.

My early experiences taught me that travel has a unique power to shape a person's perspective, to make the foreign familiar and the familiar foreign. In India, my birthplace, travel opened me to the diversity of my heritage and culture. But it was in Nigeria that I first became aware of the profound impact travel could have on my understanding of humanity. Living in Nigeria as a child exposed me to a world vastly different from the one I'd left behind in India. Nigeria was alive with contrasts—the rhythm of local markets, the infectious joy of the people, the juxtaposition of wealth and poverty, and the resilience in the face of life's daily challenges. From an early age, I realised that life was filled with complexities, and I saw how people managed to find meaning and joy even in difficult circumstances. This experience left me with a lasting impression: travel isn't simply about finding beauty; it's about discovering humanity in all its forms.

As a child, I quickly became fascinated by how travel challenged my assumptions. Nigeria was a far cry from the images of Africa I'd encountered in books or on TV, and it was humbling to witness the richness of culture and tradition that coexisted alongside modern influences. Travel brought the world to life, moving beyond abstractions and into concrete, vibrant reality. Nigeria wasn't just a place; it was a complex ecosystem of human experience, a place where I began to understand that each destination holds a multitude of stories. Every country, every city, every village offered layers of history, resilience, and lessons to be learned if only I was willing to open my mind and listen.

When I eventually moved to the United States, travel took on a different meaning. In many ways, moving to America was like moving to another world. I had become accustomed to a certain rhythm of life, one where community and cultural pride were deeply embedded into everyday interactions. Suddenly, I found myself in a society that seemed driven by individualism and ambition, where my heritage felt like both a badge of honour and an occasional barrier. The act of "travelling" here wasn't just about adjusting to a new place; it was about adapting to a new cultural landscape, one that was foreign to me despite its superficial familiarity. Here, I learned a different form of resilience—the resilience required to retain one's identity in the face of pressure to conform.

Travel also showed me the nuances of human connection, how each place has its own social codes and rhythms. In America, I learned how important it was to understand these codes and to respect them, even if they didn't align with my own. I experienced moments of subtle racism and faced feelings of being an outsider. But these challenges forced me to grow, teaching me the value of self-reflection and adaptability. In every moment of discomfort, there was a lesson, and with every person I encountered, there was an opportunity to learn.

Moving to Australia brought yet another layer of complexity to my understanding of travel and identity. In Australia, I began to appreciate travel as an ongoing journey of self-definition. It was liberating to realise that identity isn't static; it evolves with every place I visit, every person I meet, and every experience I have. Here, I embraced my identity as a global citizen, someone who didn't belong to just one place but to many. Travel taught me that identity is as layered as the places we visit, and that each new place offers the chance to redefine who we are and who we want to be.

Looking back, I see how each country shaped my worldview in distinct ways, challenging my assumptions and broadening my understanding. Travel was more than just a series of relocations—it was a process of shedding and gaining layers, each experience leaving its mark on my heart and soul. It taught me that the world is both big and small, that people everywhere share the same fundamental needs and desires, yet express them in beautifully unique ways. It was this understanding that made me crave further exploration, pushing me to seek out places that would challenge and expand my sense of self even more.

Through these journeys, I came to understand that travel has the power to transform us in unexpected ways. It's not just the grand adventures that leave a mark; it's the small, seemingly ordinary moments—the unexpected conversations with strangers, the first taste of a new cuisine, the sight of a landscape that defies words. Each of these moments is a thread in the fabric of a larger story, one that weaves together all the places we've been and the people we've met along the way. Travel isn't just about discovering the world; it's about discovering ourselves within it, about realising that each new experience, no matter how small, is an opportunity to grow.

It's easy to view travel as a way to escape, to disconnect from the stresses of daily life. But for me, travel has always been about immersion. It's about stepping outside of what I know and into what I don't, about pushing beyond the boundaries of familiarity and comfort. Travel has never been about collecting stamps in a passport or ticking destinations off a list. Instead, it's been about collecting experiences, each one a building block in my understanding of life, purpose, and connection.

The true power of travel, I've found, lies in its ability to remind us of our shared humanity. In each place I've visited, I've been reminded that no matter how different we may seem on the surface, there are threads that bind us all. The warmth of a smile, the comfort of a shared meal, the universality of laughter—these are the things that bridge the gaps between cultures and bring people together. Travel teaches us to see beyond differences, to appreciate the commonalities that unite us, and to celebrate the diversity that makes each place unique.

Travel, I believe, is a lifelong journey—a journey of curiosity, discovery, and growth. It is a journey that takes us not only across geographical borders but across the borders of our own minds and hearts. Every new place offers a new way of seeing the world, and with it, a new way of seeing ourselves. And so, with each trip, I find myself transformed, a little closer to understanding who I am and what I am here to do.

As I continue this journey, I am reminded that travel is, in many ways, a journey towards purpose. Each step I take, each place I visit, brings me closer to the realisation that purpose isn't something we find in a single moment—it's something we build, piece by piece, as we embrace the unfamiliar and allow it to change us. Through travel, I have found a sense of purpose that is rooted not in accomplishments but in connections, not in destinations but in the journey itself.

Chapter 2
THE EARLY YEARS: LESSONS FROM NIGERIA AND INDIA

My earliest memories of travel are rooted in Nigeria. Living in a developing country as a child exposed me to a world vastly different from the polished images often depicted in Western media. Nigeria was a place of striking extremes, where wealth and poverty coexisted in unexpected proximity. The bustling markets were filled with vibrant colours, aromas, and sounds that seemed to dance in the air, drawing people from diverse backgrounds together. Each person in those markets carried a unique story, a unique struggle, and a unique hope. And just a few streets away, I witnessed poverty that was not hidden but was a part of the landscape, woven into the city's identity.

It was here in Nigeria, in these early years, that I first began to understand the depth of human resilience and the strength people carried with them. Nigeria had a way of teaching life's toughest lessons with both subtlety and force. The contrasts in the environment were more than physical; they were philosophical and emotional, challenging my young mind to reconcile how such contrasts could coexist. I saw resilience in children who found joy in simple games, kicking makeshift footballs down dusty roads, crafting toys out of discarded scraps, and building worlds of imagination where materials were scarce. Even with limited resources, the children radiated an energy that was infectious, their laughter echoing down the streets as they chased each other through the markets and alleys.

Through these early experiences, I learned that life is rarely fair, and yet, in this unfairness, there is a powerful dignity. I saw adults who had every reason to be bitter but chose to be hopeful, people who found meaning in community and joy in small moments, despite the obstacles they faced daily. I witnessed individuals who displayed an unbreakable will to make the best of what they had, an attitude that struck me as both admirable and humbling. They taught me that happiness, hope, and fulfilment weren't luxuries afforded only to those with material wealth. Instead, these qualities were often nurtured in those who, despite hardship, held on to values like family, community, and faith.

It wasn't long before I realised that my time in Nigeria was shaping my perspective on life. I began to see that travel wasn't simply about moving from one place to another; it was about immersing oneself in the heartbeat of a new environment and understanding the people who lived there. Nigeria became my first real lesson in empathy, in the power of seeing beyond appearances to the spirit and strength within. It taught me to look for humanity's core, beyond wealth, status, or comfort.

When my family travelled back to India, where I was born, I experienced another kind of cultural education. India was both familiar and foreign to me—a land I had roots in but also a place I had grown distant from. As a young child, I'd absorbed fragments of my heritage, but living in other countries had shaped my worldview in unique ways. Returning to India offered a chance to connect with the traditions, values, and history that defined my family's culture. India's diversity, its seamless blending of ancient customs with modernity, felt as vast and intricate as the country itself.

In India, I witnessed a way of life that was different yet had similarities to what I'd seen in Nigeria. Here, spirituality was woven deeply into the fabric of everyday life, guiding people through hardships and joys alike. It was striking to see how people seemed to embrace both suffering and happiness with a kind of acceptance that was unfamiliar to me at the time. Every ritual, from morning prayers at sunrise to the lighting of incense in temples, felt deeply connected to something bigger than the individual self. Life in India carried a spiritual rhythm that felt timeless, like a melody passed down through generations. It was clear that, for many, existence wasn't merely about the material or the tangible; it was about seeking a higher purpose, about connecting to something eternal.

This exposure to India's spirituality planted the seeds of a lifelong quest for understanding my own purpose. I began to see that people could find meaning not just in personal achievement but in the search for something transcendent, something beyond the self. Witnessing how spirituality was seamlessly integrated into daily routines, I was struck by the realisation that life's trials and tribulations weren't seen as obstacles but as parts of a greater journey. There was a humility, a grace, in the way people approached both joy and sorrow. They didn't separate the two; instead, they embraced both as essential aspects of a fulfilled life.

These early travels laid the foundation for my lifelong love affair with exploration, adventure, and learning from other cultures. Nigeria had shown me resilience, the kind of resilience that thrives even in the most challenging conditions. India, on the other hand, offered me a perspective of inner strength—a strength rooted in faith, tradition, and an unwavering sense of purpose. Between the two countries, I found a balance of both external and internal resilience, a duality that has guided me through my life and my journeys since.

Travelling back and forth between Nigeria and India, I began to see the world as a mosaic, a collection of cultures, histories, and human experiences that were interconnected yet distinct. Nigeria and India taught me that while the world may be vast and varied, there are universal values that bind us together. The concept of family, of community, of finding purpose in the face of adversity—these were constants across borders. And I began to see myself as a citizen of the world, belonging not to a single place but to each place that had left a mark on my soul.

As I grew older, I held on to these early lessons. Nigeria taught me to never underestimate the strength and resilience of people, to recognise that wealth is often found in human connection rather than possessions. India showed me the beauty of living with purpose, of grounding oneself in faith, and of finding meaning in everyday moments. These were lessons that shaped my worldview, guiding me as I navigated new countries, met people from diverse backgrounds, and confronted challenges along the way.

Reflecting on those early years, I realise that Nigeria and India gave me something invaluable: a foundation for understanding the world in a way that goes beyond surface-level differences. They showed me that, despite varied cultures and unique circumstances, people everywhere share the same basic desires for love, hope, and purpose. These foundational lessons prepared me for a life filled with travel, a life where each new place was a chance to build on the values I had learned as a child.

To this day, the memories of Nigeria's markets and India's spiritual landscapes remain vivid in my mind. They serve as reminders of the resilience and dignity that can exist even in difficult circumstances.

They remind me to approach each journey with humility, open-mindedness, and a desire to connect. And they fuel my belief that travel, at its core, is about learning to see the world—and ourselves—more clearly, through the lens of shared human experience.

Chapter 3

THE COMPLEXITIES OF IDENTITY: AMERICA AND AUSTRALIA

Moving to the United States during my formative years felt like stepping into another world. I had grown up across continents, exposed to Indian traditions, the lively energy of Nigeria, and the intricacies of navigating these vastly different environments. But America introduced me to a cultural landscape that was distinct from any I had experienced before. Assimilating into American culture was itself a journey—one that challenged me to balance my Indian heritage, my Nigerian experiences, and the norms and expectations of this new society.

In many ways, America was a place of opportunity, but it also came with the expectation of assimilation. The drive to fit in felt ever-present, particularly for someone like me who already carried a mixture of cultural influences. I remember my first days at an American school, feeling the weight of expectation and the desire to find my place. From the way I spoke to the way I dressed, I became acutely aware of the small things that marked me as different. This awareness grew sharper when I encountered moments of subtle racism—instances where a casual remark or a passing glance reminded me that, in some people's eyes, I was an outsider. These moments were jarring, but they also brought a valuable lesson: in a place as diverse as America, everyone was both an insider and an outsider in some way.

These experiences tested my sense of self and my resilience. I was torn between the pressure to adapt and the need to preserve my identity, my heritage, and the values that my family had instilled in me. I learned to navigate this tension by adapting in ways that didn't compromise my core identity. I embraced aspects of American culture that resonated with me while holding on to the facets of my heritage that were meaningful. Over time, I grew more comfortable with being different. I began to see every challenge as an opportunity for growth and every experience of feeling out of place as a reminder of my unique perspective.

In America, I also encountered a strong sense of individualism—a value that contrasted with the collective mindset I had grown up with in India and Nigeria. In the United States, the idea of self-reliance and personal ambition was woven into the fabric of everyday life. This perspective taught me to be self-motivated, to set goals, and to work towards them with determination. But it also led me to reflect on the value of community, something that was deeply ingrained in me from my early experiences. I realised that while individual achievements were celebrated, there was also a quiet strength in the communities that people built around shared values and goals. Balancing these two perspectives—the individualistic and the communal—became a part of my evolving identity.

Years later, when I moved to Australia, I found myself once again adapting to a new environment. Australia was, in many ways, a fusion of the experiences I had already known, yet it was unique in its own right. It had the openness of America but with a more laid-back, egalitarian approach. The social landscape was different; there was a blend of cultures, a respect for diversity, and a slower pace that allowed people to connect more naturally. For the first time, I felt a sense of ease in navigating my identity. Australia welcomed my difference as part of its multicultural fabric, allowing me to embrace my heritage while fully participating in a new society.

In Australia, I also found a refreshing sense of balance. Unlike the fast-paced, hyper-individualistic culture of America, Australians placed high value on work-life balance and community involvement. This perspective allowed me to view my identity through a new lens, one where I could appreciate the journey rather than focusing solely on the destination. Australia's emphasis on nature, the outdoors, and a more relaxed lifestyle taught me to slow down, to savour life, and to appreciate the small moments. Living here reinforced the idea that success didn't need to come at the cost of personal well-being or happiness.

Throughout my journey in Australia, I embraced my identity as a global citizen—someone who belonged everywhere and nowhere at the same time. Living in different countries had instilled in me the resilience to view change not as a threat but as an opportunity to broaden my perspective. Each place I had called home shaped my understanding of the world in distinct ways, adding new layers to my sense of self. By the time I reached Australia, I began to see identity not as a fixed set of characteristics but as a living, evolving process. Each experience, each connection, and each lesson left its mark, shaping me in ways that were both subtle and profound.

It was liberating to realise that identity isn't something we are simply born with; it is something we create through our interactions, our choices, and our willingness to grow. Being a "global citizen" meant that I no longer felt bound by a single cultural narrative. Instead, I saw myself as a part of multiple narratives, each one contributing to a richer, more complex sense of who I was. This realisation gave me the freedom to move beyond labels and expectations, to embrace my differences, and to find strength in the diversity of my experiences.

The concept of identity also became more nuanced for me in Australia. I began to understand that I didn't have to compartmentalise my experiences or choose one culture over another. Each layer of my identity—Indian, Nigerian, American, and now Australian—was a piece of a larger puzzle. I no longer felt the need to justify my background or to make it fit neatly into a single box. Instead, I embraced the idea that identity is fluid, shaped by each place, each person, and each experience. Australia helped me see that identity is not about conforming to one mould; it is about integrating all the pieces of our story into something unique.

Living in Australia also allowed me to look back at my journey with a sense of gratitude. I felt fortunate to have experienced life in such varied cultural settings, each one offering a different perspective on what it means to belong. My journey taught me that identity is not just about where you come from; it's about where you've been, what you've learned, and how those experiences shape the way you see the world. Each new place brought with it a new lesson, a new way of understanding myself and others.

Ultimately, the complexities of identity that I encountered in America and Australia taught me that our sense of self is never static. It is a dynamic, ever-changing process that grows with each new experience and each new relationship. Identity, I realised, is about embracing both our roots and our wings, allowing each experience to deepen our understanding of who we are and who we can become.

In reflecting on my journey across these diverse landscapes, I came to appreciate the beauty of embracing a multi-faceted identity. America and Australia both challenged me, albeit in different ways, to navigate my own complexities and to find my place in an ever-evolving world. Today, I carry a piece of each country with me, a reminder of the resilience, adaptability, and openness that each place instilled in me. I no longer see myself as bound by a single culture or identity; instead, I see myself as part of a global tapestry, woven together by the people, places, and experiences that have shaped my life.

Chapter 4

THE MIDDLE EAST: A JOURNEY THAT CHANGED EVERYTHING

By the time I embarked on my journey to the Middle East, I had already experienced the transformative power of travel in many parts of the world. Yet, nothing prepared me for what I would encounter in this complex, deeply historic region. With its ancient cities, rich cultures, and unique political landscapes, the Middle East was unlike any place I had been before. I thought I knew what travel could teach me, but the Middle East opened my eyes to an entirely new level of depth, resilience, and humanity.

The beauty of the Middle East doesn't just lie in its landscapes or architecture; it lives in the contradictions, the strength, and the grace of the people who call it home. This trip became a turning point, not just because of the physical sites I visited but because of the internal journey it sparked. Travelling through Syria, Iraq, and Lebanon was as much about understanding myself as it was about discovering the culture and people of these remarkable places.

Before we set off, my wife had understandable concerns. Her reservations echoed the fears many hold about travelling to a region often associated with conflict, danger, and instability. She wondered why I was so intent on going to a place the news often painted as hostile and volatile. I had no easy answer, except that I had long believed the places that scare us or make us uncomfortable are often the ones that have the most to teach us. And I was right. This trip was not simply a holiday; it was a transformative journey of self-discovery, pushing me beyond my comfort zones and challenging my beliefs about resilience, kindness, and purpose.

Lebanon was our first destination. Unlike Syria and Iraq, Lebanon's history of conflict had played out over a longer span, and the country was marked by the echoes of civil wars, invasions, and political instability. But even with this turbulent past, Lebanon's people welcomed us with kindness and warmth. Walking through Beirut, I saw a city of contrasts—modern skyscrapers standing beside ancient ruins, bustling markets, and neighbourhoods marked by bullet-riddled buildings. Lebanon was alive with energy, a fusion of the old and the new, East and West, hope and despair.

In Lebanon, my wife and I had one of the most profound experiences of our lives. We were taken hostage by a group who mistook us for foreign agents due to a misunderstanding. The experience was harrowing, pushing me to the limits of fear, patience, and resilience. It tested my strength and forced me to confront the idea of mortality in a way I never had before. Strangely, amidst the fear, there was also a moment of clarity. I realised that life, with all its uncertainties, was a gift, and that purpose was not something to be chased but something to be lived in every precious moment we are given.

After hours of questioning, we were finally released, and the men who had detained us even apologised. As we left, I felt a mix of gratitude and bewilderment, realising that even in such an extreme situation, there had been moments of humanity. I couldn't forget the man who offered us water or the one who assured us that we would be safe. This experience underscored for me the fundamental truth that, regardless of circumstances, people are capable of kindness, and that often, the hardest situations bring out the deepest connections.

Our second destination was Syria. Entering the country was surreal, marked by border crossings, military checkpoints, and the visible scars of recent conflicts. The first thing that struck me was the resilience of the people. In cities like Damascus, I was overwhelmed by the warmth and openness of locals who greeted us with smiles and a willingness to share their stories, despite the hardship they had faced. Syria's history is a blend of ancient splendour and modern tragedy. As we walked through the streets of Damascus, the oldest continually inhabited city in the world, I was struck by the layers of history—the ancient markets, the grand mosques, and the remnants of recent destruction.

One evening in Damascus, we joined locals for tea in a small café that had, miraculously, remained intact through years of war. Sitting there, I realised that life went on in ways I hadn't expected. People chatted, laughed, and enjoyed the company of friends and family. Despite the fear and uncertainty that had become a part of daily life, there was a remarkable ability to find joy and meaning in the present. This resilience wasn't limited to physical survival; it was about an unbreakable spirit, a determination to live fully in whatever circumstances fate had dealt. It was humbling, and it made me realise that purpose often lies not in avoiding hardship but in rising above it.

From Syria, we travelled to Iraq. The journey into Iraq was equally eye-opening, but with a new set of complexities. Iraq's history is a blend of ancient civilisation, from the cradle of Mesopotamia to recent struggles that have left many of its cities scarred. We visited Baghdad, a city that still held the echoes of its days as a centre of the Islamic Golden Age. Despite the destruction and devastation of recent decades, the spirit of the place was undeniable. It was here that I felt a profound connection to history, a sense of walking in the footsteps of countless generations who had built, nurtured, and loved this land.

In Iraq, I saw villages that had been rebuilt from rubble, people who had been displaced multiple times but had found ways to rebuild their lives. Walking through streets where houses still bore bullet holes, I witnessed the strength of those who had lived through unimaginable loss and yet had chosen hope over despair. They didn't wear their hardships as a burden but as a badge of survival. Conversations with locals revealed a common theme: life was fragile, but it was also precious. People spoke of their families, their dreams, and their aspirations, much like anyone else, but there was an added layer of appreciation—a gratitude for the present moment that I had rarely encountered before.

Each encounter across these countries reaffirmed a universal truth: that human beings are capable of extraordinary resilience. I met people who had lost homes, family members, and stability, yet they found ways to continue, to laugh, and to dream. Their strength was a reminder that purpose isn't about having a perfect life; it's about finding meaning in the life you have, about continuing to move forward even when the odds seem insurmountable.

The architecture, the culture, the food—everything in the Middle East felt like a testament to the human capacity to create beauty even amidst adversity. The stunning mosques, ancient ruins, and historic marketplaces stood as symbols of resilience, each one bearing witness to the endurance of countless generations. These structures were not only beautiful but resilient, surviving wars, invasions, and natural disasters. They reminded me that resilience is not just an individual trait but a collective one, a strength that grows from shared experiences, shared history, and shared hope.

In the Middle East, I saw that life's value isn't measured by the absence of hardship but by how one responds to it. Every person I met, every story I heard, added to my understanding of what it means to live with purpose. Purpose, I realised, isn't about grand achievements or accolades. It's about the quiet strength to carry on, the willingness to love even when love seems scarce, and the courage to hope in the face of uncertainty.

This journey through the Middle East fundamentally changed the way I understood my place in the world. It taught me that purpose isn't found in comfort or safety but in facing life's challenges head-on. The people I met and the experiences I had became a part of me, shaping how I see the world and my role in it. The resilience, warmth, and determination of the people I encountered became guiding principles in my own life, reminders that even in the most challenging circumstances, we can find beauty, strength, and meaning.

When I returned home, I carried with me the lessons learned from the people of the Middle East. I realised that resilience isn't just about enduring hardship; it's about finding purpose and meaning in every moment. My experiences in Syria, Iraq, and Lebanon taught me to approach life with a sense of gratitude and a commitment to live each day fully. The challenges I had faced in the corporate world, the personal struggles, and the moments of self-doubt all felt different now, viewed through the lens of resilience and gratitude I had gained in the Middle East.

Travelling through these regions not only expanded my understanding of the world but also deepened my connection to my own life. I no longer viewed purpose as a destination, something to be achieved or earned. Instead, I saw it as a journey, a daily commitment to living with integrity, compassion, and resilience. The Middle East had taught me that true strength comes from embracing life in all its complexities, from recognising that every experience, whether joyful or painful, adds a layer of depth to our existence.

Looking back, this trip was far more than an adventure. It was a journey into the heart of human resilience, a journey that stripped away the superficial and revealed the raw, beautiful essence of life. I returned with a profound sense of humility, a deep gratitude for the life I have, and an unwavering belief in the importance of kindness, compassion, and connection. And as I continue on my own journey, I carry these lessons with me, hoping to honour the resilience and strength of the people I met by living my life with the same courage and purpose.

Chapter 5
THE BEAUTY OF HUMANITY AND THE REALITY OF DANGER

Travel often conjures images of breathtaking landscapes, ancient wonders, and unforgettable experiences. But what happens when travel brings us face-to-face with danger, forcing us to confront the darker sides of human existence? This question came to life for me during one of the most harrowing experiences of my journey—the day we were taken hostage by Hezbollah in Lebanon. This experience could have left me fearful, shattered my love for travel, and marked the end of my desire to explore unknown lands. But, strangely enough, it did the opposite. It became a catalyst for resilience, a turning point that taught me invaluable lessons about the fragility of life, the resilience of the human spirit, and the incredible ways that purpose can emerge in the most unexpected places.

When I recall that experience, what stands out is not just the fear, but the way it brought into sharp focus the beauty of human connection even in the bleakest moments. The day began like any other, with plans to explore the sights and sounds of Lebanon's vibrant culture. But as we ventured into Dahiyeh, a Hezbollah stronghold, we found ourselves suddenly in a position of vulnerability, with our lives no longer entirely in our own hands. Taken by Hezbollah members due to a misunderstanding, we were interrogated, questioned, and held in a place where no one knew our whereabouts or the outcome of the ordeal.

In those tense hours, my senses were heightened, my mind racing through every possible scenario. The idea that something so ominous could unfold in the midst of what was supposed to be a journey of discovery forced me to examine the nature of risk and the strength it takes to keep moving forward in the face of fear. At times, I wondered how we would get out, what the outcome would be, and how this would affect my wife, who had already been apprehensive about visiting this part of the world. In those hours, I felt the vulnerability of being a human in an unpredictable world, but I also felt a deep connection to my own inner strength, the same strength that we each carry but rarely need to access.

Oddly enough, while we were in their custody, I also witnessed acts of humanity from the very people holding us. One man, seeing the distress on our faces, offered us water, a simple gesture that felt profound given the circumstances. Another man reassured us, telling us that we would be safe. Even in a situation clouded by fear and uncertainty, there were moments that reminded me of the kindness that exists in people, regardless of context. In these small but significant gestures, I saw humanity, the shared thread that connects us all, regardless of our backgrounds, beliefs, or circumstances. It was a reminder that even within an environment of tension and hostility, acts of empathy and compassion can emerge.

This experience left me forever changed. While the initial days following our release were filled with a mixture of relief and disbelief, I soon began to reflect on what this ordeal had taught me. First and foremost, it reinforced that life is indeed fragile. There is a tendency to believe that the world is a safe place, that our plans and routines protect us from the unpredictable. But when you are stripped of control and placed in a situation where survival is no longer a guarantee, you become acutely aware of life's tenuous nature. It's an awareness that can either paralyse you with fear or empower you with a newfound appreciation for every moment, every relationship, every small act of kindness.

For me, the latter was true. Returning home after this experience, I realised that resilience is about far more than simply surviving hardship. Resilience is about finding meaning within those hardships, about facing life's darkest moments and allowing them to teach us, strengthen us, and broaden our perspectives. It's about recognising that our greatest growth often emerges not from comfort but from discomfort, from moments that challenge our sense of stability and force us to confront who we are at our core. This experience could have easily made me more cautious, fearful, and reluctant to travel. But instead, it did something remarkable—it reignited my commitment to live purposefully, to continue seeking out experiences that challenge my worldview, and to embrace every part of life, both the beautiful and the difficult.

This ordeal was a profound reminder that our purpose in life is often shaped by how we respond to adversity. We can't avoid hardship entirely; life will test us, sometimes in ways we cannot foresee. What defines us, however, is not the adversity itself but how we choose to respond. I could have allowed the experience with Hezbollah to instill in me a lasting fear of the unknown, to make me wary of stepping outside my comfort zone. But I chose, instead, to see it as a lesson in resilience and perspective. This was a reminder that purpose isn't just about the goals we set or the achievements we pursue; it's about our capacity to remain open to life's lessons, even in its darkest moments.

Reflecting on this experience, I've come to believe that true growth often requires us to confront the parts of the world—and ourselves—that make us uncomfortable. It's easy to stay within the familiar, to surround ourselves with places, people, and situations that reaffirm our beliefs and values. But real growth happens when we allow ourselves to be challenged, when we place ourselves in situations that force us to reckon with uncertainty and confront the limits of our understanding. This experience was a reminder that travel, at its core, is not simply about seeing new sights; it's about expanding our inner landscape, about embracing both the beauty and the darkness of the world.

After Lebanon, I felt a deeper appreciation for the complexity of humanity. People are not simply "good" or "bad." Just as I had seen acts of kindness within an experience that was, on the surface, terrifying, I realised that people everywhere are shaped by their circumstances, beliefs, and experiences. This understanding deepened my empathy and taught me to approach the world with a more open heart and mind. I saw that even those who may seem like "the other" are not so different from ourselves, that beneath the surface, we all share the same need for connection, respect, and understanding.

Since this experience, I have approached life with a renewed sense of purpose. I no longer view resilience merely as the ability to endure; I see it as the strength to find meaning in life's hardships, to let every experience, whether joyful or painful, add to my understanding of what it means to live fully. This experience with Hezbollah showed me that even in the face of adversity, there is an opportunity for growth, a chance to learn about the depths of my own courage and the power of empathy.

In the end, this ordeal didn't shatter my love for travel; it strengthened it. I returned home with a greater commitment to exploring the world, not just for its beauty but for its complexities and contradictions. I now travel not just to see the sights but to seek out the lessons that each new place, each new encounter, can offer. I travel to deepen my understanding of myself and the world, to confront the darkness and embrace the light, knowing that both are essential parts of the journey.

The experience with Hezbollah reaffirmed that life is both fragile and resilient, a blend of vulnerability and strength. It reminded me that our purpose lies not in avoiding discomfort but in embracing it, in facing life's challenges with courage and openness. And as I continue to travel, to seek out new experiences, I carry this lesson with me: that real growth, real resilience, comes from confronting the parts of the world—and ourselves—that make us uncomfortable. Through these experiences, we discover the true beauty of humanity and the profound strength within ourselves.

Chapter 6
TRAVEL AS A PATH TO SELF-DISCOVERY

Travel, for me, has never been just about crossing destinations off a list or capturing beautiful photos. It is, at its essence, a journey within. Each place I've visited and every culture I've encountered has shown me new facets of myself, challenging my beliefs and reshaping my understanding of what it means to live a meaningful life. In every landscape, from bustling cities to quiet mountain villages, I've found echoes of my own thoughts, fears, and dreams, reflecting back to me in ways that bring clarity and growth.

When I first started travelling, I didn't consciously think of it as a path to self-discovery. Like many people, I was initially drawn to travel out of curiosity and a desire to see new sights. But over the years, as each journey brought me into contact with different ways of living, new beliefs, and unfamiliar customs, I realised that travel was slowly chiselling away at my preconceived notions, making me question who I was and what mattered most. travelling forced me to confront parts of myself that I might have ignored or taken for granted had I stayed in the familiar surroundings of home.

In every new environment, I found myself adapting—not only to external conditions but also to different perspectives. In some places, I was treated as a stranger, a novelty, or an outsider, which initially left me feeling unsettled, but eventually helped me see the beauty in belonging nowhere and everywhere at once. The more I travelled, the more I realised that being a "global citizen" isn't about losing your identity but expanding it. Each journey became a way to piece together a broader understanding of humanity, one that transcends borders and cultural differences.

One of the most profound lessons I've learned through travel is that purpose is not something we stumble upon; it is something we create. Often, we think of purpose as a fixed destination—a goal we must achieve, a calling we must follow. But I've come to understand that purpose is fluid, shaped by the places we visit, the people we meet, and the experiences we embrace. Each journey I've taken has added a layer to my sense of purpose, reinforcing the idea that life isn't about reaching a single destination. Instead, it's about the richness of the journey itself, the accumulation of moments, insights, and connections.

Travel has taught me to embrace change, to be comfortable with the unknown, and to see beauty in uncertainty. In every new place, I've been reminded that life is constantly evolving, that who I was yesterday may not be who I am today, and that this constant evolution is something to be celebrated, not feared. Each journey has been an invitation to let go of rigid expectations and to open myself to whatever the world has to teach. In doing so, I have found freedom—the freedom to be myself, unbound by societal norms or personal limitations.

One of the most transformative aspects of travel is the opportunity to immerse oneself in different cultures. Language barriers, different customs, and unfamiliar landscapes force us to shed our assumptions and open ourselves to new ways of thinking. In Japan, I learned the value of mindfulness and attention to detail; in India, I was reminded of the strength found in community and family bonds. In Nigeria, I discovered resilience and creativity among people who faced challenges I could hardly imagine. Each culture offered a new lens through which to view the world, teaching me that there is no single way to live, love, or find happiness. These experiences have made me more adaptable, more empathetic, and more willing to embrace life's unpredictability.

What I've come to realise is that travel isn't just about discovering the world—it's about discovering ourselves within it. There's a profound difference between the person I was before I began to explore the world and the person I am now. Travel has shown me strengths I didn't know I possessed, weaknesses I needed to address, and potential I hadn't tapped into. In every interaction, every new landscape, and every challenging moment, I've come face-to-face with my own humanity, my own limitations, and my own capacity for growth. It's a humbling process, one that has made me appreciate the complexity of the world and my place within it.

Through travel, I've also learned that purpose is less about grand achievements and more about the small, everyday choices we make. Purpose is found in the conversations with strangers, the kindnesses exchanged, and the courage to step out of one's comfort zone. It's found in the moments of laughter shared over a meal in a foreign city, the silent awe of standing before an ancient monument, and the sense of connection that transcends language and cultural differences. Each of these moments has added to the tapestry of my life, reminding me that purpose is an accumulation of small experiences that together create a life of meaning and fulfillment.

One particular memory stands out in this journey of self-discovery. I was hiking alone in the mountains of Peru, surrounded by breathtaking vistas and the quiet majesty of nature. As I walked, I felt an overwhelming sense of peace—a connection to something larger than myself. In that moment, I understood that purpose doesn't require validation from others; it doesn't require titles, accolades, or societal recognition. Purpose is deeply personal, and it is something we feel most profoundly when we are true to ourselves. Standing on that mountainside, I felt my place in the world, not as an individual seeking to conquer it, but as a part of something vast and beautiful, something that exists beyond the boundaries of my own life.

Travel has also taught me that self-discovery is an ongoing journey, one that doesn't end when we return home. Each trip has left an indelible mark on me, carrying lessons that continue to shape my decisions, my relationships, and my outlook on life. The experiences I've gathered from around the world have become a part of who I am, influencing how I respond to challenges, how I view success, and how I define happiness. The sense of purpose I feel now is not about reaching a final destination but about living each day with intention, curiosity, and gratitude.

Now, as I look to the future, I feel a strong desire to share these stories and insights with others. I want others to know that they, too, can step outside their comfort zones and discover the extraordinary potential within themselves. Travel has given me a gift—a gift of perspective, resilience, and an unquenchable thirst for learning. I hope that by sharing these stories, I can inspire others to embark on their own journeys of self-discovery, to see the world not just as a collection of destinations, but as a path to understanding who they are and what they are capable of.

If there's one message I hope readers take from my journey, it's that self-discovery is not a linear path. It is a winding road, one filled with unexpected twists, challenges, and rewards. Each person we meet, each culture we immerse ourselves in, adds a new chapter to our story, helping us understand the depth of our own humanity. By embracing the unfamiliar, we uncover layers of ourselves that we didn't know existed. Through travel, I've found not just my purpose, but an ever-evolving sense of self, one that grows richer with each experience and each connection.

In the end, travel has shown me that purpose is not a destination we reach but a journey we undertake. It is a continuous unfolding, a journey that teaches us to see life in all its complexity, beauty, and fragility. The world is a vast and magnificent place, full of lessons waiting to be learned. And as I continue to explore it, I carry with me the knowledge that the greatest discovery we can make is within ourselves.

Part 2
THE MIDDLE EASTERN ADVENTURE

Chapter 7

APPREHENSION AND EXCITEMENT: PLANNING THE JOURNEY

I t all started in Sydney. By 2023, I had been working in a job that, at first, felt like a good fit, but the longer I stayed, the more it began to wear on me. I was growing restless, feeling the kind of discomfort that only comes when you know something in your life needs to change. It wasn't just about work, though—this was deeper. As an only child, I had always found ways to keep myself entertained, to seek out new challenges, and to embrace change whenever I felt it was needed. And in January of 2023, I could feel that familiar itch. I needed to get away, to break free from the routine. I was ready to go somewhere—anywhere. I would have lived on Mars if it were possible.

My wife, Veema, however, is my opposite in so many ways. Where I embrace the unknown, she prefers the familiar. So, one evening, when I told her I was thinking about a big change, she suggested I sit down and watch a travel documentary. Maybe it would scratch the travel bug without actually having to go anywhere. She probably thought it was a safe bet to curb my wanderlust for a bit, but it ended up having the opposite effect.

The documentary was about Aleppo, Syria—a place I hadn't given much thought to before. The film showed a group of travel bloggers visiting the war-torn city. I remember seeing footage of children playing football in the streets, the backdrop of their game a haunting landscape of bombed-out buildings. But what struck me most wasn't the devastation; it was the resilience of the kids. They were using a ball that wasn't even a real football—it looked hard, like it was made of stone. And yet, they kicked it around with so much joy, as if they didn't have a care in the world. It was an image that wouldn't leave me, and as I sat there watching, I felt something stir inside me.

I turned to Veema and gave her the look—the one that she knows means I've made up my mind. "I'm going to the Middle East," I told her, "and I'm going to Syria. I want to go to that exact spot." I could see the fear in her eyes. I knew she wasn't going to be easily convinced. She had every reason to be scared—the news coming out of Syria and the surrounding region was enough to make anyone think twice. And while I would never force her to come with me, I also knew I couldn't resist the pull. I had to go.

Her response, however, was one I won't forget. She said, "I'll come with you. But what happens if ISIS or some terrorist group comes after us?" In my usual, somewhat naive, way of trying to lighten the situation, I replied, "Veema, you run left, I'll run right. One of us might get killed, but the other will survive and keep the lineage going." It was a terrible joke, and not the reassurance she needed, but it was all I had in the moment.

Veema wasn't convinced—at least not at first. For months, she resisted the idea, standing firm in her fear of what could happen. But slowly, I wore her down. I used every bit of charm and persuasion I had, and eventually, she agreed to come with me. I knew deep down that she wouldn't have let me go alone, but still, her agreement felt like a victory.

With her on board, I threw myself into planning the trip. I contacted fixers in Syria, Iraq, and Kurdistan—locals who could help us navigate the complexities of travelling in the region. Every detail of the itinerary excited me: the places we'd see, the people we'd meet, the stories we'd come back with. It was shaping up to be the adventure of a lifetime.

Meanwhile, life in Sydney continued on as normal. In March, I made another significant decision: I resigned from my job. It had been a long time coming. I had been feeling increasingly disconnected from the culture of the company, and the more I stayed, the more it reminded me of the bullying I had endured as a child. The behaviours I was witnessing at work—condescension, passive aggression, subtle racism—had become unbearable. It was the second company in a row that didn't align with my values, and I knew it was time to move on.

That April, Veema and I took a trip to Fiji and Vanuatu. It was a much-needed escape from the grind, and while it was far less daunting than what we had planned for the Middle East, it was still a reminder of why I love to travel. Fiji and Vanuatu were stunning, but I couldn't help but notice how these islands were already feeling the effects of climate change. Whole communities were beginning to sink into the ocean, and the people, while incredibly friendly and welcoming, were living with the knowledge that their homes were disappearing.

One experience from that trip stands out. We visited a volcano in Vanuatu and stood just a few metres away from molten lava spitting from its depths. It was one of those surreal moments where you feel so small in the face of nature's power. It was the kind of adventure that would satisfy most people's need for excitement, but for me, it only fueled my desire for the Middle East.

By September, we were back in Melbourne, where I had started a new job. But again, something didn't feel right. The corporate world, once so appealing, was starting to feel hollow. Every day brought new frustrations and the same old toxic behaviours that had driven me away from my previous job. It was clear that this wasn't where I belonged.

Around this time, the war between Israel and Palestine was escalating, and Lebanon was getting drawn into the conflict. One night, as we sat down for dinner, I turned on the TV and saw our foreign minister, Penny Wong, warning Australians not to travel to Lebanon. "Any Australians still in the country should leave immediately," she said. My wife looked at me, her eyes wide with concern. "What do we do now?" she asked. Without missing a beat, I replied, "A warning is just a warning. It's up to us to decide what we're going to do."

Despite everything we were seeing on the news—Hezbollah's threats, Israel's retaliations—I couldn't shake the feeling that we needed to go. It wasn't fear of what might happen that concerned me. It was the fear of not going, of missing out on this opportunity to see a part of the world so few people dared to visit. And so, we pressed on with our plans. No one would insure us, but we found some questionable travel insurance anyway. I didn't even register our trip with the Australian government. We were going, come what may.

By November, everything was set. We packed our bags, double-checked our itinerary, and prepared ourselves for the unknown. It was time to leave, and despite the warnings and the risks, I felt nothing but excitement. Our adventure was about to begin.

Chapter 8

THE JOURNEY BEGINS — MELBOURNE TO LEBANON VIA QATAR

December arrived, and with it, the moment we had been planning and quietly anticipating for months. This trip, the one that felt like a leap into the unknown, was finally here. My wife and I had agreed not to share the full truth with our families. We didn't tell them we were going to places like Syria or Lebanon, places that would send them into a panic. Instead, we chose a safer narrative. We told them we'd be visiting the Middle East but stuck to safer destinations: Kuwait, Bahrain, Qatar. It wasn't entirely false—those were places we could have easily visited. But in reality, we were taking a gamble with this trip, and we weren't sure how it would turn out.

This wasn't going to be a quick getaway. We had planned for four to five weeks of travel, knowing it would take time to absorb everything we were about to experience. As the date approached, a mix of excitement and apprehension built up inside me. I wasn't afraid of what might happen—I was more eager than anything else— but there was a weight to it all. We were about to step into places that most people only hear about on the news, and the stories from those places were rarely good. But that's exactly why I wanted to go: to see it for myself, to understand what life was like for the people living there, and to witness firsthand the beauty that persists, even in places of conflict.

We left Melbourne, the familiar city that had been our home, and flew to Qatar. Our first stop was a safe one—Qatar, a country known for its wealth, luxury, and relatively stable political situation. It was the perfect place to start, a soft landing before the real adventure began. In Qatar, we spent a few days exploring, and while it was impressive, it felt like a warm-up for what was to come. We visited the World Cup stadiums, strolled through Souq Waqif, and wandered through the Falcon Souq, where birds of prey are treated like royalty. It was all a fascinating glimpse into the culture of the Gulf, but my mind was already looking ahead.

As we moved through our days in Qatar, there was a quiet anticipation hanging in the air between my wife and me. We both knew that the easy part was ending, and we would soon be heading to Lebanon, a place that carried its own risks, especially given the ongoing conflict. But this trip wasn't about comfort; it was about pushing boundaries—our own, and the ones set by the world around us.

After a few days of rest and sightseeing in Qatar, the time came for us to board the plane to Lebanon. I remember settling into my seat and feeling a sense of both relief and excitement. The real trip was about to begin. I had seen so many maps of the region in my planning, but watching our plane's flight path as we neared Lebanon was something else. Due to the ongoing conflict, the plane couldn't fly over Israel directly, so we had to take a detour around it. I kept my eyes on the screen, following the plane's route as it curved away from Israel and out over the water.

For some reason, I couldn't stop watching the map, tracing every move. As we neared Israel's airspace, the plane began to bank. I glanced out of my window on the right side of the aircraft, and there it was—Gaza. In that moment, something shifted in me. I could see Gaza, Palestine, and Israel stretching out below, and it struck me how close I was to one of the most volatile, conflict-ridden places in the world. From up there, it looked peaceful—just a stretch of land, bathed in the light of the setting sun. But I knew what was happening below. I knew people were dying there, families were being torn apart, and lives were being shattered. And here I was, sitting comfortably on a plane, flying to Lebanon with the freedom to go wherever I pleased.

It was a moment of profound dissonance. How lucky was I, I thought, to be born into a life where I had choices, where I could sit on a plane and go wherever I wanted. And how unlucky were the people just below me, trapped in a cycle of violence and destruction with no way out. The thought hit me hard, and I couldn't shake it.

I began to reflect on the people I interacted with back home—colleagues in the corporate world, some of whom had bullied me, belittled me, or undermined me. What would they think if they could see this? If they could witness the fragility of life the way I was seeing it now? Would they still be so caught up in their own arrogance, in their quest for power and control? Would they still treat others so poorly if they knew how easily everything could be taken away?

It was a moment of clarity for me. In that instant, as I looked down at Gaza, I realised how small and insignificant our day-to-day struggles can be in the grand scheme of things. We spend so much time chasing after money, status, and material success, but all of that becomes meaningless in the face of true hardship. When survival becomes the only goal, everything else fades into the background. It made me question the choices we make in life. Why do we hurt others when it's so easy to be kind? Why do we waste time on petty squabbles when life itself is so fragile?

As the plane curved away from Gaza, I watched as the land slipped out of view, and we began our approach to Lebanon. My thoughts followed the plane as it straightened out, flying over the sea, and I found myself feeling a strange mixture of sadness and gratitude. Sadness for the people below who had no choice but to endure the horrors of conflict, and gratitude for the life I had, for the freedom I so often took for granted.

The pilot's voice crackled over the intercom, announcing our descent into Beirut. The sun was setting as we made our final approach, casting a warm glow over the Mediterranean. Lebanon awaited, and with it, the unknown. As we touched down, I took a deep breath, feeling a sense of peace despite everything. We were here. The journey had truly begun.

Chapter 9

DISCOVERING LEBANON: BEAUTY, HISTORY, AND SORROW

Arriving in Lebanon felt like stepping into a world where beauty and hardship coexist in a delicate balance. From the moment we touched down at the Beirut airport, it was clear that this trip would be unlike any other. The city greeted us with rain, and the airport was partially flooded—an unexpected welcome—but that hardly mattered. We were in Lebanon, and there was an energy to the place that I hadn't experienced before.

Our driver, Mohammed, was waiting for us, smiling despite the puddles of water we had to wade through to get to the car. Mohammed was part of the Hezbollah political party, which added an intriguing layer to our experience. Despite the tension that name evokes, Mohammed's energy was cheerful, even warm. It was hard not to like him immediately. His happiness seemed unshaken by the realities of the country's political struggles. He exuded a resilience that would come to define much of what we saw in Lebanon—a people who had learned to smile through decades of hardship.

We checked into our cozy hotel in Beirut, and the next morning, we met our tour guide. The sun was shining, the air felt fresh, and there was a palpable sense of excitement. Lebanon is small, but it contains multitudes—from ancient cities to modern chaos, from mountain monasteries to Mediterranean beaches, from sorrow to joy. Over the next few weeks, we would explore a land that had seen the rise and fall of empires, yet continued to stand, scarred but beautiful.

Baalbek: The Colossal City of the Gods

One of our first major stops was Baalbek, an ancient city that felt as if it had been ripped from the pages of mythology. Situated in the Beqaa Valley, Baalbek is home to some of the most well-preserved Roman ruins in the world. Its sheer scale is overwhelming, and yet, when we arrived, there were only five or six tourists wandering the massive grounds. It was as if the world had forgotten this place, but standing there, I knew I would never forget it.

The most striking structure in Baalbek is the Temple of Jupiter. It's impossible to describe its immensity without standing beneath the towering columns, each one carved from stone blocks weighing tons. Once the largest temple in the Roman Empire, it was designed to impress the gods themselves. Today, it still commands awe. The craftsmanship, the sheer audacity of building something so grand, reminds you of how insignificant modern architecture can feel in comparison.

As I wandered through the ruins, I couldn't help but think about life, resilience, and purpose. These ruins had seen centuries of worship, war, and decay, and yet here they stood—silent witnesses to the ebb and flow of history. I found myself reflecting on my own life, how the struggles I've faced seemed both monumental and trivial against the backdrop of something this ancient.

In many ways, Baalbek felt like the embodiment of Lebanon: a place scarred by conflict but still standing, still magnificent. And yet, as grand as it was, we had the place almost entirely to ourselves. The world seems to have forgotten about Baalbek, but perhaps that is what makes it even more special—a hidden treasure, waiting to be rediscovered.

Byblos: The Birthplace of Civilisation

From Baalbek, we moved to Byblos, another UNESCO World Heritage site. Byblos is one of the oldest continuously inhabited cities in the world, and walking its streets is like stepping into the very heart of human history. The Phoenicians, the Crusaders, the Ottomans—they all left their mark on this city. Byblos has been many things over the millennia: a bustling port, a religious centre, a place of learning. It was also the birthplace of the Phoenician alphabet, the precursor to most modern scripts.

We wandered through the ancient souks, their narrow streets lined with shops selling everything from handmade crafts to antiques. The city exudes a charm that is both old and new. I remember watching the sunset over the Mediterranean from the harbour, the sky ablaze with colours that seemed almost too vivid to be real. There, standing by the sea, I felt the weight of history settle around me.

Byblos is a city of layers. Every street, every wall, every building holds a story. And as I stood in its citadel, gazing out at the sea, I realised that this city, like Lebanon itself, was a testament to resilience. It had survived countless invasions, occupations, and disasters, yet it continued to thrive.

Sidon and Tyre: Phoenician Legacy and the Call of the Sea

Our journey took us further south, to Sidon and Tyre—two cities that had long been on my list of must-see places. Sidon, with its iconic sea castle, is a city of ancient maritime power. The

Phoenicians, those legendary sailors and traders, built their empire from here, spreading their influence across the Mediterranean. The sea castle, perched on a small island just off the coast, was built by the Crusaders in the 13th century and stands as a symbol of Sidon's rich history.

We walked across the narrow causeway to the castle, the sound of the waves lapping against the stones echoing through the air. From the top of the castle, you can see the entire city, the sea stretching out endlessly to the horizon. There's something humbling about standing in a place like this, where the past feels so close you could almost touch it. I thought about the Phoenician sailors who had once launched their ships from these shores, venturing into the unknown, just as we were venturing into the unknown on this journey.

Further south, we arrived in Tyre, a city that once rivalled Carthage and Rome. Tyre is less visited than it deserves to be, perhaps because of its proximity to the Israeli border and the tensions that still simmer in the region. But Tyre is a gem, a place where the layers of history are so rich, you can practically feel them under your feet.

The Roman Hippodrome in Tyre is one of the largest and best-preserved in the world. As I stood in the stands, I imagined the chariot races that had once taken place there, the roar of the crowd, the dust kicked up by the horses as they thundered around the track. It felt like a scene straight out of *Gladiator*, and once again, I was reminded of the parallels between Lebanon's past and its present. The people of Lebanon, much like the ancient Phoenicians and Romans, have endured—through invasions, occupations, and wars—yet they remain, resilient and proud.

Baalbek to Beirut: Contrasts and Reflection

After visiting these ancient cities, returning to Beirut felt like coming back to the modern world, but even in the capital, history looms large. Beirut is a city of contradictions. It is beautiful and chaotic, vibrant and broken, all at once. The scars of the 2020 port explosion were still fresh when we visited, and the damage was a stark reminder of the fragility of life here. But Beirut's spirit is unbroken. The Blue Mosque, standing tall amidst the city's skyline, is a symbol of this resilience. Its minarets soar into the sky, and its interior is as beautiful and serene as any mosque I've ever visited.

One afternoon, we wandered into the mosque's courtyard, and I was struck by the peacefulness of the place. A group of pigeons was hopping around, and for some reason, I felt the urge to jump with them. My wife filmed it in slow motion, and for a few seconds, it was as if time itself slowed down—just me, the birds, and the quiet serenity of that moment in Beirut.

Kadisha Valley and the Monasteries of Qozhaya

One of the most moving experiences in Lebanon was our visit to the Kadisha Valley, where ancient Christian monasteries are carved into the cliffs. The valley is a UNESCO World Heritage site, and it's easy to see why. The rugged beauty of the landscape is breathtaking, and the sense of isolation and devotion that permeates the area is palpable.

We stayed at the Saint Anthony Monastery in Qozhaya, one of the oldest monasteries in the world. Built into the rock, the monastery has been a place of refuge and worship for centuries. There's something humbling about staying in a place like this, where time seems to stand still, and the worries of the modern world fade away. I spent time reflecting in the quiet halls of the monastery, thinking about the monks who had lived here through centuries of war, occupation, and hardship. Their faith, like the monastery itself, seemed unshakable.

The Journey Through Lebanon: Lessons in Resilience

As we travelled through Lebanon, from Baalbek to Beirut, from Sidon to the Kadisha Valley, I couldn't help but be struck by the resilience of this small but mighty country. Lebanon is a land that has been shaped by its past—its beauty and its sorrow are intertwined. It's a place where history isn't just something you learn about in books; it's something you see, feel, and breathe in every corner, in every stone, in every person you meet.

Lebanon is a country that refuses to be defined by its hardships. It's a place where people continue to live, love, and find joy, even in the face of incredible adversity. And as a traveller, I found myself humbled by the strength of the Lebanese people, by their ability to smile and laugh, even when the weight of their country's history seems almost too heavy to bear.

This journey through Lebanon was more than just a sightseeing trip. It was a lesson in resilience, in beauty, in sorrow, and in hope. And it was a reminder that no matter where we go in the world, we are all connected by our shared humanity, by our desire to find meaning and purpose in the lives we lead.

Chapter 10

THE GENEROSITY OF STRANGERS — KINDNESS IN THE HEART OF LEBANON

One of the most remarkable parts of our journey through Lebanon was the generosity we encountered from everyday people. Lebanon is a country that has been shaped by hardship, by war, and by political and economic instability, yet what stood out the most wasn't the difficulties its people faced—it was their overwhelming kindness. It's something you don't often see in the fast-paced, individualistic cultures of the First World. In Lebanon, people may have very little, but they offer what they have freely, with open hearts and genuine smiles.

I'll never forget the old man we met in one of the souks. He had a small shop selling sweets, and as we wandered past, he caught our eye and waved us inside. Without hesitation, he started telling us about his life, his family, and the history of his little shop. His eyes lit up as he spoke, his pride in his work and his homeland clear in every word. He didn't ask for anything in return, but instead, insisted on giving us free sweets—delicate, honey-soaked baklava and ma'amoul, stuffed with dates and nuts. The sweetness of the pastries paled in comparison to the sweetness of his spirit.

It was a pattern we'd see over and over again. In another souk, we met a young boy pushing a massive wheelbarrow piled high with bread. He couldn't have been more than ten years old, but he was already part of the fabric of the community, helping to provide for his family by selling bread in the market. He approached us shyly, offering us some of the fresh, warm flatbread from his cart. We bought a piece, of course, but the boy insisted on giving us more for free, laughing as he handed it over. His simple joy in sharing something so basic was humbling.

In Tripoli, a city that often carries a reputation for danger, we met people who welcomed us as if we were old friends. One evening, we found ourselves in a shisha café, surrounded by locals puffing away on water pipes, chatting, laughing, and arguing in rapid Arabic. Before long, a group of strangers invited us to join them, sharing their shisha with us as though we were family. They asked where we were from, told us about their lives in Lebanon, and offered insights into the complexities of the region, all while passing the pipe and cups of sweet mint tea. Their warmth and hospitality erased any preconceptions we might have had about the city.

Another day, we stopped at a small kebab stand for lunch, expecting to pay for our meal as usual. But the owner, a middle-aged man with a kind face and a warm smile, refused to take our money. "You are guests in my country," he said, waving away our attempt to pay. "It is my pleasure to serve you." We insisted, but he was adamant. He packed up more food than we could possibly eat, wrapping it carefully and handing it to us with a grin. The generosity of these people—people who often had very little to give—left me speechless.

This generosity wasn't just a one-off experience; it was everywhere we went. From the souks of Beirut to the mountain villages, from Tripoli to Tyre, people welcomed us with open arms, offering us food, stories, and laughter. It was a reminder that even in places where life is hard, the human spirit can shine through in the most beautiful ways. Lebanon's people have an innate kindness, a warmth that transcends the hardships they face, and it left a lasting impression on me.

Kadisha Valley: Faith and Solitude in a Sacred Place

One of the most profound experiences of our time in Lebanon was our visit to the Kadisha Valley, a UNESCO-listed site that has been a place of refuge and spirituality for centuries. The valley is home to a series of ancient Christian monasteries, many of them carved into the mountainsides, and it is a place where hermits and monks have lived in solitude for centuries, seeking closeness to God through isolation and prayer.

We made our way to the **Saint Anthony Qozhaya Monastery**, where we had planned to spend a night. As we arrived, the air felt different—calm, serene, almost sacred. The monastery, perched high in the mountains, overlooked the valley, and the landscape stretched out before us in a breathtaking panorama. Rocky cliffs, dense forests, and winding paths gave the place an almost biblical feel, as though time had stood still here for centuries.

That evening, as we sat down to dinner, we met a monk who had come into the dining hall. His presence was quiet, unassuming, but something about his manner drew me in. As we began to talk, I noticed something familiar about his accent. "Where are you from?" I asked. "Sydney," he replied with a smile, though he quickly added, "But I am Lebanese." He told us that he had once worked as an executive at one of Australia's big four banks, earning a half-million-dollar salary. "But it wasn't the life for me," he said. "I felt lost, like I had no purpose. So I left it all behind and came here."

I was fascinated by his story. Here was a man who had lived the life that so many people in the corporate world aspire to—high salary, prestige, power. And yet, he had chosen to leave it all behind to live in a monastery in the mountains, seeking a simpler, more meaningful existence. As he spoke, I couldn't help but think about my own journey, the decisions I had made to leave behind a life that no longer felt fulfilling. His story resonated deeply with me.

The monk took us on a tour of the monastery, showing us the caves where some of the hermits lived. These men had been here for decades, disconnected from the modern world, living in silence and contemplation. The caves were small, dark, and simple, with little more than a bed, a small altar, and a few personal items. It was hard to imagine a life like this—so detached from the chaos of the outside world—but there was something undeniably peaceful about it. These men had found their purpose in solitude, and there was a purity to it that I admired.

Chapter 11
DAHIYEH: THE START OF THE HEZBOLLAH ADVENTURE

As we left Kadisha Valley, a thought occurred to me. We had seen the beautiful, ancient, and serene sides of Lebanon, but there was another side to the country that I was curious about—the side that the news so often focuses on. As we were driving with our driver, Mohammed, I turned to him with a question that had been lingering in my mind. "Can we visit Dahiyeh tomorrow?"

Dahiyeh is a suburb of Beirut, and it is controlled by Hezbollah. It is a place that most tourists avoid, and for good reason. Hezbollah is a powerful political and military group in Lebanon, but it is also classified as a terrorist organisation by several countries, including the United States. Visiting a place like Dahiyeh wasn't part of the typical tourist itinerary, but I felt compelled to see it for myself. Lebanon is more than just its beautiful landscapes and historical sites—it is a country with a complex political and social fabric, and I wanted to understand it from all angles.

Mohammed looked at me, his expression a mix of surprise and curiosity. "Why do you want to go to Dahiyeh?" he asked. I explained that I wanted to see all sides of Lebanon, not just the ones that were safe and comfortable. "I want to understand what it's like there," I said. "I've seen the beauty, the history, the generosity of the people. But I also want to understand the other side."

Mohammed hesitated for a moment, then nodded. "Okay," he said. "We can go."

This was the beginning of what would become one of the most intense and eye-opening parts of our journey in Lebanon—the start of the Hezbollah adventure. I knew that by going to Dahiyeh, I was stepping into a world that most tourists would never see, a world that existed in the shadows of Lebanon's vibrant cities and stunning landscapes. But I also knew that if I was going to understand this country, I had to see it all—the good, the bad, the beautiful, and the dangerous.

And so, with Mohammed as our guide, we prepared for the next leg of our journey.

Chapter 12

THE HEZBOLLAH ENCOUNTER – KIDNAPPED IN DAHIYEH

The next morning, we left the peaceful serenity of Kadisha Valley behind, our hearts racing with anticipation. Our destination for the day was Beirut—a city of contrasts, both ancient and modern, beautiful yet scarred by its turbulent history. But before we fully immersed ourselves in the capital, I had requested something different, something a bit more dangerous. I wanted to see Dahiyeh, the stronghold of Hezbollah.

I'll admit, my adrenaline-seeking nature had led us to some pretty wild places before, but this was different. Hezbollah, a powerful political and military group, controlled this part of Beirut, and it wasn't a place most tourists ventured. My wife, who had grown accustomed to my need for adventure, was less thrilled, though she put on a brave face. Joining us was another tourist—just as eager as I was to see the less-travelled side of Lebanon. Our driver, Mohammed, who was a member of the Hezbollah political party himself, promised to take us on a brief tour of the area before we moved on to explore the city.

As we descended from the winding hills and valleys, the air changed. Beirut sprawled out before us, the city's chaos and vibrancy visible in every corner. The tension in the car was palpable as we approached Dahiyeh, a neighbourhood that felt worlds away from the rest of the city. This wasn't the Beirut of bustling cafés and lively souks—this was a different reality.

Mohammed pointed out the change almost immediately as we entered Dahiyeh. The streets were narrower, the buildings more run-down. Yellow Hezbollah flags lined the streets, their unmistakable symbol fluttering in the wind. I spotted posters of the group's leader, Hassan Nasrallah, his stern face staring down from walls and street corners, flanked by other political leaders from Lebanon and Iran. The imagery was stark—a reminder of the region's complex and often dangerous political landscape.

As we drove deeper into the neighbourhood, the atmosphere became even more somber. We passed a memorial wall covered in photographs of fallen soldiers. Mothers and brides sat beside the pictures, weeping for their loved ones who had died in the wars. It was a sobering sight—a visceral reminder of the cost of conflict.

The streets of Dahiyeh had an eerie stillness to them, a stark contrast to the lively, bustling parts of Beirut we had seen earlier. It felt like a different world, one defined by tension and struggle. The poverty was visible everywhere, from the crumbling buildings to the dilapidated infrastructure. Dahiyeh was a ghetto in every sense of the word, and the weight of its history was heavy in the air.

Despite the unease, my curiosity got the better of me. I asked Mohammed if we could stop somewhere for coffee and shisha, hoping to get out of the car and soak in the atmosphere a bit more. He glanced at me through the rearview mirror and shook his head. "Not yet," he said. Being part of Hezbollah himself, he knew the area well and understood the potential dangers better than we did. His refusal only heightened the tension.

We continued driving, taking in the scenes around us, unsure of what to expect. At one point, Mohammed turned to us with a cheeky grin and asked, "Do you want to see a place that no one goes to?"

Before anyone else could respond, I immediately answered, "Yes, please." This was exactly the kind of thrill I had been seeking—a glimpse into the hidden corners of a place most people wouldn't dare explore.

Mohammed made a sharp right turn, and we found ourselves on a deserted street. The air felt heavier here, the silence more profound. As we drove further, I caught sight of a building that stood out from the rest—gleaming, pristine, and completely out of place. It looked almost surreal, like the White House in Washington, D.C., dropped in the middle of this rundown neighbourhood.

"What is that?" I asked, my eyes glued to the massive, glowing structure.

"That," Mohammed replied, "is the Pavilion. It's where Nasrallah gives his speeches that are broadcast around the world—on BBC, CNN, and all the networks."

I was both awestruck and excited. This was the heart of Hezbollah's operations, a place few outsiders had ever seen. As we drove past the Pavilion, one of the tourists in the car took out a camera and snapped a photo of the building.

That's when everything changed.

Out of the corner of my eye, I noticed a group of men sitting at the base of the Pavilion, watching us intently. They hadn't moved before, but the moment the camera clicked, they sprang into action. Within seconds, their heads turned sharply in our direction, and a sense of dread settled in the pit of my stomach.

We continued driving, but the tension in the car had escalated. Just as we rounded a corner onto the main street, a motorbike roared up beside us, blocking our path. Everything happened so fast it was hard to process. The man on the motorbike dismounted, walked calmly up to our car, and without a word, reached into the driver's side window. He removed the key from the ignition, effectively immobilising us.

The next thing I knew, he had taken our passports and our phones. Without saying a word, he stepped back, standing behind the car with our belongings in hand. My heart pounded in my chest. This wasn't part of the adventure I had imagined. We were stuck, and the gravity of the situation began to sink in.

That's when the real fun began.

The Interrogation Begins

The tension was palpable. We had been sitting in that car for hours, unsure of what was really happening, but trying our best to remain calm. At first, the situation felt manageable, almost routine—an unexpected security check, maybe a misunderstanding about the photograph one of the tourists had taken. But as the minutes stretched into hours, the atmosphere shifted. What started as an adrenaline-pumping curiosity about visiting Hezbollah's stronghold in Dahiyeh had turned into a slow-burning realisation that we were no longer in control of our circumstances.

After the motorcyclist blocked our car and took our passports and phones, we were left helpless in the hands of our driver, Mohammed, and a handful of strangers who had appeared from nowhere. Mohammed, calm as ever, assured us repeatedly that everything was going to be fine. "Leave it with me," he said confidently, stepping out of the car to negotiate with the man who had stopped us. His membership in the Hezbollah political party seemed to grant him a degree of familiarity with these people, but that didn't ease our growing sense of unease.

I tried to focus on anything but the situation. The bustling street around us was alive with activity, a strange contrast to the quiet tension inside the car. On the right, a small bookshop buzzed with customers; on the left, a café hummed with conversation and clinking cups. Life went on outside, oblivious to the uncertainty and anxiety building inside our vehicle. Time ticked by. Twenty minutes turned into thirty, then into an hour. Mohammed returned to the car periodically to reassure us, but his words were starting to feel hollow.

Two hours passed. Still no passports. Still no phones. The sun beat down on the car, and we were sweating, both from the heat and the growing realisation that this was more than a simple security check. Mohammed eventually came back and said we were waiting for someone else to arrive, another person who needed to verify something as part of the "standard procedure." By now, two more motorbikes had shown up, and the group of men standing behind our car had grown larger. One of the new arrivals, an older man with a long beard and a serious demeanour, looked experienced—like someone who had seen situations like this unfold before. I couldn't shake the feeling that we were no longer in a casual situation. This was becoming something far more serious.

At the three-hour mark, Mohammed came back to the car and told us that we needed to go somewhere. He didn't explain where, just that it was part of the process, and everything would be fine. Then, out of nowhere, two black Audis appeared, flanking our car on either side, while motorbikes surrounded us from the front and back. It was surreal—we were being escorted through the streets of Dahiyeh as though we were some kind of VIP convoy, but nothing about this felt glamorous. In fact, it felt anything but.

I glanced over at my wife, who sat quietly beside me, her nerves more apparent with each passing minute. Our hearts were racing, but outwardly, we were trying to remain composed. In moments like this, panic wouldn't help, and so we held on to the hope that Mohammed, our guide and now our mediator, was right—that this was all just part of an overly complicated security procedure.

As we continued driving, I asked Mohammed where our passports and phones were. His response was vague—he said they might be with one of the men on the motorbikes or in one of the Audis, but he wasn't sure. That was the first real indication that even he wasn't entirely in control of the situation. We kept following the lead motorbike as it turned right, and that's when things became stranger. All of the other vehicles—the Audis and motorbikes—continued driving straight. I asked Mohammed, "Isn't the driver with our passports going straight?" He hesitated, then tried to reassure us with a half-hearted excuse, saying that they were probably going to make copies and we'd get everything back soon.

We were now driving through more secluded streets, heading towards what seemed to be a compound with security guards standing by the entrance. The gate opened for us, and we pulled into a garage. It was empty except for our car. The motorbike with the older man parked nearby, and Mohammed stepped out to have another quiet conversation with him. At this point, we had been in this ordeal for over four hours, and the reassuring words that had calmed me earlier were losing their effect.

Finally, Mohammed returned to the car with news. He told us that someone from "IT" was coming to run background checks on us, and once that was done, everything would be resolved. His explanation didn't make much sense. Why would Hezbollah need someone from IT to check our background? It was a surreal thought—imagining a bureaucratic office worker with a laptop, typing away to see if we were wanted criminals or spies.

The fifth hour dragged on. And then, just as Mohammed had promised, "the IT man" arrived. I spotted him in the rearview mirror—a man dressed entirely in black, riding up on a motorbike with a laptop bag slung over his shoulder. It was strange, almost comical, seeing this figure who looked more like a hacker from a spy movie than someone working for Hezbollah. He was led inside, and after half an hour, Mohammed came back with instructions: we were going to be questioned.

My heart sank. This was no longer just an inconvenience. We were officially being detained, and the light-hearted assurances we had clung to in the beginning now felt dangerously naïve.

"Two at a time," Mohammed said. "First, it will be you and your wife."

I looked over at my wife, and for the first time, I saw real fear in her eyes. She hadn't said much throughout the ordeal, trying to remain calm for both of us, but now it was clear that we were stepping into something much more serious than we had anticipated. Neither of us had ever imagined our trip would lead to this moment—being interrogated by Hezbollah in the heart of their stronghold.

As we stepped out of the car, I took a deep breath and prepared myself for whatever was about to come. Little did I know, things were about to get a lot more interesting.

Under Hezbollah's Watch

When Veema and I were finally led into the room for questioning, the reality of the situation hit hard. We had been sitting in the car for hours, our nerves fraying with each passing minute, but this—this was real. The room was dimly lit, sparsely furnished, with two sofas lining the walls. On one side sat the man with the long beard who had taken our passports and phones earlier, now watching us with a steady gaze. In front of us, behind a desk, sat the man in all black, clearly in charge. He was flanked by another man, this one wearing a bulletproof vest, his presence adding an air of authority to the already tense atmosphere.

As we sat down on the opposite sofa, Veema and I exchanged a glance, trying to maintain our composure. Smiling was instinctual for us, a way to ease tension in awkward situations, and in this moment, we couldn't help but offer polite smiles as we greeted the men. But their expressions remained unreadable. The interrogation began with basic questions—names, nationalities, the usual. But then came the question I had been expecting: "Why are you in Dahiyeh?"

I explained, as calmly as I could, that we were tourists, here to explore Lebanon's rich history and culture. Our driver had suggested we visit Dahiyeh, and we thought it would be interesting to see a different part of Beirut. Of course, I knew they were suspicious. Dahiyeh isn't a place tourists visit. It's Hezbollah's stronghold, and wandering through it as a foreigner without a clear reason is bound to raise alarms.

As I spoke, I noticed the man in the bulletproof vest staring at my arm. I followed his gaze and realised he had spotted my tattoos—a scorpion and a lion. Tattoos aren't uncommon, but in this setting, I could see why they might be of interest. The man leaned over and whispered something to the bearded man, who immediately reached for his phone. In a poorly executed attempt at discretion, he pretended to scroll through his phone, but it was clear he was trying to snap a photo of me. I watched as he fumbled with the camera, aiming it in my direction without even trying to hide what he was doing.

It was almost comical. The bearded man wasn't subtle in the slightest, and I could tell Veema was fighting the urge to giggle beside me. He took one shot, but apparently dissatisfied with the result, he got up and moved closer, hiding behind a set of curtains like a child playing hide-and-seek. He peeked out from behind the fabric and took another photo, his phone clicking audibly in the quiet room. It was absurd, almost surreal, and despite the tension, I couldn't help but stifle a laugh. I shot Veema a quick look, silently urging her not to laugh, but the moment was too strange to ignore.

The questioning resumed, with the man in black flipping through our passports, pausing to look at the various stamps from our travels. "You've been to many countries," he said, almost with a sense of surprise. "You're a lucky man."

I smiled politely. "I am very lucky, but I've also worked hard to make it happen." My words were measured, careful not to sound too defensive but also not too submissive. I wanted them to see me as just another traveller, someone who enjoyed seeing the world and had stumbled into their territory out of curiosity, not malice.

They continued asking about our lives—how many children we had, to which I replied none. "Inshallah," the man said with a smile, "you will have three or four children soon." Veema, who had no desire to have children, played along beautifully, nodding in agreement. "Absolutely," she said, forcing a smile. "As many as we can." It was a bizarre conversation, but in moments like these, it's all about playing the part, giving them what they want to hear without provoking suspicion.

Then came the more direct questions about the political situation. "Don't you know we're at war with Israel?" the man in black asked, his tone more serious now.

"I do," I responded carefully. "And I'm very sorry for all the lives lost." I could feel the tension rising again as he scrutinised my words. Any misstep here could make things worse, so I chose my responses with precision, acknowledging the conflict but steering clear of any controversial statements.

The questioning dragged on for over an hour, with the men checking our phones and photos, flipping through the images we had taken, all while making occasional small talk. When they were satisfied, they told us we could go. Veema and I stood, relieved to be leaving, though we knew the ordeal wasn't over yet. We returned to the car and waited while the tourist who had been with us went through her own round of questioning.

After about 45 minutes, we were called back into the room, this time with the whole group—myself, Veema, the tourist, our driver Mohammed, and our tour guide. We sat down again, facing the same three men, though now the atmosphere felt heavier, more ominous. For a long while, no one said anything. The silence was suffocating, the awkwardness stretching out like an invisible weight pressing down on all of us.

Finally, I broke the silence. "What's the status?" I asked, trying to sound casual.

The man in black didn't look up. "We're waiting for a few more people to arrive. They'll do a background check on you, and then we'll go from there."

I've learned to distrust that phrase: *we'll go from there*. It's a statement without an end, without a resolution. It's a way of stalling, of keeping you in limbo without offering any real answers. The hours passed slowly. There was some idle conversation—about children, about travel—but mostly, we just sat there, unsure of what was coming next.

At one point, the tourist, clearly worried about her expensive camera, asked the man in black not to damage it. He smiled and said, "Don't worry, we are not ISIS. We will not break your camera." His words were meant to be reassuring, but then he added with a smirk, "And also, don't worry, we are not going to kill you... yet."

The *yet* hung in the air like a lead weight. My heart skipped a beat, and I could see the fear flash across Veema's face. That one word had changed everything. We had been told repeatedly that we were safe, that this was just routine, but now, the situation felt far more precarious.

Twenty minutes later, two new figures walked into the room—a tall man, at least six foot two, and a much shorter man, probably five foot two. Both were older, maybe in their 60s or 70s, and they entered the room with a burst of energy, chatting loudly in Arabic. Despite their seemingly cheerful demeanour, I could tell they were important. These were commanders, possibly higher-ups in Hezbollah, and their presence meant things were escalating.

After a few minutes of conversation that I didn't understand, the tall man and his companion left the room. Another half-hour passed before we were told that it was time to leave. Relief washed over me, but I remained cautious. Nothing was certain yet.

As we gathered our things, I approached the man in black, offering my hand in a gesture of thanks, trying to lighten the mood with a bit of humour. "Thank you for this... interesting experience," I said, half-joking.

He looked at my hand and shook his head. "We do not shake hands," he said. "We do this." He raised his hand in a Hezbollah salute, and I mimicked the gesture, eager to end the encounter on the right note.

As we stepped outside, I noticed the two commanders waiting by the door, along with the black Audi and our own car. But there was something new—an old man, looking angry, with my red backpack slung over his shoulder. And then, there it was: a black jeep with tinted windows parked nearby, its engine idling, waiting.

My stomach dropped. We weren't out of the woods yet.

The Longest Day — Separated and Blindfolded

As we emerged from the compound, the sun already beginning to dip, I saw the tall Hezbollah commander pointing towards the large black jeep parked in front of us. His gestures were direct—he wanted my wife, the tourist, and our female tour guide to get into the vehicle. In that moment, a wave of panic gripped me. None of us spoke Arabic, and I felt a surge of dread as I realised they intended to separate us.

"This isn't right," I muttered to Mohammed, our driver. "We can't split up like this."

I suggested, perhaps foolishly, that it would be better if we split ourselves more evenly—my wife or the tour guide should go with me and Mohammed, who both spoke Arabic. I thought it would be safer that way, that someone who could communicate should be with the other half. But this idea backfired. When Mohammed translated my suggestion to the tall commander, the man just nodded and said, "No worries, all the women can go in the jeep."

My heart leapt into my throat as I watched the three women—my wife, the tour guide, and the tourist—climb into the vehicle. The door shut with a loud thud, and the jeep's black-tinted windows obscured everything inside. For the first time, my heart rate spiked, my mind racing with every terrible possibility. *You can't separate me from my wife,* I said, more to myself than to anyone around me. The tall commander noticed my unease and gave a tight smile. "Don't worry, everything will be okay."

Chapter 12 *The Hezbollah Encounter — Kidnapped in Dahiyeh*

But I didn't believe him. How could I?

Before I could do anything else, Mohammed ushered me towards our own car, now being driven by the smaller, older Hezbollah member—the one I had seen earlier in the compound, the one who had seemed angry since the moment we arrived. He had my backpack slung over his shoulder, and something about his demeanour felt off. As we climbed into the car, I felt a sudden wave of helplessness. Mohammed tried speaking to the driver, but the little guy barely responded, his face set in a deep scowl.

We pulled out of the compound, and I kept glancing back, desperate to make sure the black jeep was still following us. I had to know that my wife was close by, that we weren't about to be completely separated. But then, just as we were caught in a pocket of traffic in the hot, bustling streets of Dahiyeh, I looked behind us again, and the jeep was gone. My heart pounded in my chest, and I tapped Mohammed on the shoulder.

"Where is the jeep?" I asked, my voice thick with fear.

Mohammed spoke quickly to the little guy, but the only response was an irritated grumble, telling him to be quiet. I tried to stay calm, but my mind was racing. Every minute that passed felt like an eternity.

We drove for what felt like an endless five minutes before turning into an open space—a desolate car park, surrounded by old, crumbling apartment buildings. The area felt abandoned, the kind of place that made the hairs on the back of my neck stand up. We stopped, and without a word, the little guy got out of the car, locking it from the outside. I turned to Mohammed, my voice shaking.

"What is happening? Where is my wife?"

For the first time, I saw uncertainty in Mohammed's eyes. He sighed and said, "I don't know. I've never experienced anything like this before. I have no idea what's going to happen."

That was when the fear truly set in. If Mohammed, a member of Hezbollah himself, had no idea what was going on, how could I possibly predict what might happen next? My pulse quickened. The sweat on my skin felt cold as I tried to process the situation. My wife was gone. I had no idea where she was or what was happening to her. And now, even our driver—the one person I had trusted in all of this—was just as lost as I was.

Minutes later, I heard the screech of tyres behind us. I turned to see the black jeep pulling into the car park. Relief flooded my chest—at least for a moment. The jeep stopped abruptly, and the door swung open. The little guy, still seething with anger, stormed towards me, yanking open the car door and grabbing me by the arm. He dragged me out of the car and threw me onto the pavement. I hit the ground hard, my heart now pounding at 110 beats a minute. This was it, I thought—this is when things get really bad.

But before the situation could escalate further, the tall commander appeared. He stepped out of the black jeep, his presence commanding, and immediately yelled something at the little guy in Arabic. Though I couldn't understand the words, I could feel the weight of his anger. I could only imagine what he was saying—*Don't touch him. This could be a big diplomatic problem.* Whatever the words were, they worked. The little guy backed off, releasing my arm. The tall man then motioned for me to get into the jeep.

I hesitated, glancing inside, but I saw no sign of my wife. "Where is my wife?" I demanded, my voice shaking.

The tall man offered the same empty reassurance. "Don't worry. Everything is all right."

I stared at him, knowing I could no longer believe a word he said. Mohammed, sensing my hesitation, leaned towards me. "You'd better get in," he warned. "Or this could get ugly."

Chapter 12   The Hezbollah Encounter — *Kidnapped in Dahiyeh*

With no other choice, I climbed into the jeep. Mohammed followed, and the little guy slid in beside us. We sat in the backseat, the silence between us heavy with tension. Then, without warning, they put a blindfold over my eyes.

My world went black.

Before they pulled the blindfold tight, I quickly checked my heart rate. It had jumped to 110. My mind was racing, and I knew things were spiralling out of control. The curtain they hung in front of me felt suffocating, and the jeep was eerily soundproof. All I could hear was my own breathing, and Mohammed's, as we drove. I had no idea where we were going. It felt like we were trapped in a dark tunnel, both physically and mentally, isolated from the world.

For the next twenty minutes, I sat in that black silence, the uncertainty gnawing at me. Fear settled in my bones, heavier with each passing moment. When we finally stopped, the door opened, and the tall man removed my blindfold. I stumbled out of the jeep, blinking in the sudden light. We were in the underground parking garage of what looked like a dilapidated apartment building.

The tall man pointed to the stairs. "Go up," he commanded, his voice leaving no room for argument.

Terror gripped me as I asked the only question that mattered. "Where is my wife?"

He didn't even hesitate in his response. "All good," he said dismissively, waving me towards the stairs.

I turned to Mohammed for reassurance, but his face was unreadable. He simply nodded, urging me forward. I climbed the stairs, my legs heavy with fear. At the top, the door opened to reveal a man with a scanning device, like something you'd see at an airport security checkpoint. He gestured for me to remove my watch, which I did without hesitation.

As I handed it over, I noticed the little guy—the one who had taken my backpack earlier—standing behind me. His frustration was clear as he demanded in Arabic what to do with the bag. One of the guards, a tall, younger man with a beard, casually told him to leave it. Without a word, the little guy threw the bag to the ground and left. That was the last time I would see him.

I stepped further into the apartment, the weight of everything pressing down on me. I went through the scanner and was led into a small room. To my surprise, the tour guide was sitting there, but the look on her face was one of pure terror. Her normally vibrant skin was pale, drained of colour. She looked ghostly, as if the life had been sucked out of her. I approached her cautiously, asking what had happened.

"Nothing," she whispered, her voice shaky. But the haunted look in her eyes said otherwise.

From the corner of my eye, I noticed two men dressed in black, seated behind large computer screens. Five minutes passed in silence before one of them spoke. "How are you feeling?" he asked, his voice cold and detached.

"Not great," I replied. "Where is my wife?"

The man barely looked up. "I don't know."

Fear stabbed at my chest. "What do you mean, you don't know?"

He shrugged, indifferent. "We'll see."

And so the questioning began again. It felt endless—one set of interrogators would come in, ask the same questions, and then leave, only for another set to take their place. Where was I from? Why was I in Lebanon? Why had I visited Dahiyeh? Over and over, the same questions, the same answers. It was clear they were trying to see if my story would change.

In the next room, I could hear Mohammed's voice, answering his own set of questions. Were we being kidnapped? Was this just an extended interrogation? I didn't know anymore. All I knew was that I had no control over what was happening. At this point, it didn't feel like we were going to be let go. The hours dragged on—ten, eleven, twelve hours.

I felt exhausted. The weight of the situation was crushing me, but then, suddenly, a sound broke through my fear. From the room next door, I heard it—a giggle, unmistakably my wife's giggle. Relief flooded through me, my heart rate slowly settling. She was alive. She was nearby.

I asked one of the men, "Is that my wife?"

He nodded. "Yes."

"Can I see her?"

"No."

I didn't press further. Knowing she was alive was enough for the moment.

The questions kept coming, cycling through new faces, new tones. But none of it mattered anymore. My only focus was finding a way out of this situation with my wife safe by my side.

As the sun set outside, casting long shadows through the windows, I glanced at the tour guide beside me. This strong, independent Lebanese woman who had navigated us through so much now looked utterly defeated. Her voice shook as she whispered, "I just want my mommy."

Hearing those words from someone who had always seemed so tough, so in control, made the gravity of the situation hit me even harder. For the first time, I truly thought, *we're fucked*.

But still, I looked at her, trying to keep my own panic at bay. "Don't worry," I said, trying to sound convincing. "Everything will be okay. Trust me."

And then, just when it seemed like the ordeal would never end, I finally met the leader himself.

Face to Face with Nasrallah — The End of the Ordeal

The moment he entered the room, I felt it. His presence was undeniable, like the air itself had shifted. The energy changed, the tension thickened. You know how sometimes a person enters a room, and without saying a word, they command attention? This was one of those moments. I looked up, and there he was—the leader of Hezbollah himself, Hassan Nasrallah.

For months before our trip, I had seen him on the news back in Australia, almost every day. His speeches, his movements, and his decisions shaped the politics and tensions of the Middle East. Everything he did rippled through the region, and I remember wondering if his next move might disrupt our plans in Lebanon. Now, here he was, standing in front of me. This was the man who had the power to turn my entire trip—and my life—upside down.

Nasrallah was calm but firm, exuding a quiet authority. His gaze landed on me, and he didn't break eye contact. It was clear that I was now at a pivotal moment in this entire ordeal. I could feel it in the weight of his presence, the way he carried himself. He was here to make decisions about my fate, and I knew better than to take it lightly.

He didn't speak English, so the tour guide had to translate everything he said. He addressed me directly, his voice quiet but sharp. "You have three choices," he said, staring straight at me. "You could be set free. You could be killed. Or you could go to an underground prison, and no one will ever hear from you again. Which option would you like?"

There was no hesitation in my response. "I'd love to go free."

He gave a small nod, but I knew this wasn't over. There were three questions I had to answer, and I had to get them right. I could feel that in the way he framed the situation—this was a test, and if I failed, it wouldn't end well.

The first question came, his tone serious. "Did you know we are at war with Israel?"

I nodded and replied, "Yes."

His next question was sharp and to the point. "Did you know that your Australian government said, 'Do not come to Lebanon'?"

Again, I responded, "Yes."

Then came the third question, the one that cut straight through the tension. "Why the fuck did you come to Lebanon?"

That hit me hard, and the use of the F word was not lost in translation. My tour guide, clearly uncomfortable, hesitated as she repeated the question back to me. For a split second, something in me snapped. A familiar feeling took over—the same feeling I had when I faced life-threatening moments in the past. My mind raced through memories of having a gun in my mouth, nearly dying in a plane crash, and being bullied. This was just another moment in a long series of survival situations I had endured.

I looked at him, and something in me clicked. "Listen," I said, and I could feel the tension in the room shift. "I came to Lebanon to experience your culture, your people, and the beauty of your country. Yes, I know you're at war, but I grew up in Nigeria during a military coup. I've experienced violence and fear firsthand. I've been kidnapped before, and I've had a gun in my mouth. Trust me, this isn't actually that bad. What you're doing to me now? It's nothing compared to what I've been through."

I paused, letting my words sink in. I had no idea how Nasrallah would react, but something inside me told me to keep going.

"I've spent a week in your country, and I've loved every moment of it. Lebanon is my favourite place in the world. No matter what you've done to me today, I still love this country. So, if you're done with the questioning, let us go. And if you're not, can you hurry up? I've got a few more things to tick off my list before I leave this beautiful place."

The room fell silent. The tour guide looked at me like I was insane, unsure if she should even translate my words. But I urged her to go ahead, and she did. As she spoke, I watched Nasrallah's face closely. His expression softened. He smirked, then let out a small chuckle. There it was—the connection I had hoped for. He stared at me for a solid ten seconds, which felt like the longest ten seconds of my life.

Then, without a word, he stood up and walked out of the room.

As the door closed behind him, the tension broke. My tour guide turned to me, her eyes wide. "Are you crazy?" she asked, her voice filled with disbelief.

I shrugged, trying to lighten the mood. "Well, it can't get any worse, can it?"

About fifteen minutes later, the door swung open again, and my heart skipped a beat. Standing in the doorway was my wife, smiling like she had just returned from a pleasant afternoon. She looked completely relaxed, almost giddy, and I couldn't believe my eyes. "What are you so happy about?" I asked, incredulous.

She beamed at me. "I had the best time with Hezbollah!"

My jaw dropped. "What do you mean?"

"They were so sweet," she explained. "They offered me food, water, and when they asked me to stand against the wall for a photo, they said, 'Say cheese!'"

I couldn't believe what I was hearing. "Are you kidding me? When they took my photo, I asked if I should say cheese, and they told me, 'Do not.' How were they so relaxed with you?"

She just shrugged, still smiling, and I realised that she had no idea how dangerous the situation had really been. In a way, I was relieved. She had been in her own world, blissfully unaware of what could have gone wrong, and that was probably for the best.

Not long after, the tourist who had been with us was brought back into the room. Her face told a completely different story. She looked traumatised, pale, and shaken. She had clearly not enjoyed the same hospitality as my wife.

Then, in a bizarre twist, about fifteen Hezbollah members filed into the room. They lined up in front of us and apologised. "We are very sorry for what has happened today," one of them said. "You have to understand, we are at war. Today is a day of mourning in Lebanon, and no one was supposed to be out. You came to the wrong place at the wrong time, and you did the wrong thing by taking a photo of the Pavilion. We had to be sure you were not spies."

I looked at the young man with the beard, the one who had been with us since the beginning. "I don't blame you," I said. "You did what you had to do. You were being reasonable given the circumstances. If anything, I blame myself for being here in the first place."

They offered us food and water, but we declined. We just wanted to leave. They returned our passports, phones, and even my watch, and finally, we were free to go.

One by one, we were escorted back to the car park where the whole ordeal had begun. First, I climbed into the black jeep with Mohammed. The tall commander was driving, and for once, the curtain separating the backseat from the front wasn't fully closed. I could see where we were going, and though I didn't say anything, I quietly noted the path we took.

After about 20 minutes, we arrived at the same car park where, hours earlier, I had been thrown onto the street. Mohammed turned to me and whispered, "Do you know where that place was?"

I nodded, laughing under my breath. "Yeah, because they forgot to close the curtain properly. What a group."

We both chuckled, finally able to release some of the tension that had built up over the last 14 hours. It had been an insane ordeal—one filled with fear, uncertainty, and more than a few surreal moments—but it had taught me a lot. About resilience, about fear, and about life itself.

Finally, the jeep returned with my wife, the tourist, and the tour guide. We were all exhausted, mentally and emotionally drained. But we were safe. We had made it out. And as we stood there, catching our breath and trying to process everything that had just happened, I turned to the group and said, "Let's go get completely smashed."

We spent the rest of the night in a shisha bar, smoking away the stress and laughing at the absurdity of it all.

Chapter 13
MY REFLECTION

It's easy to think you know what fear feels like until you find yourself sitting in a darkened room, facing men whose actions hold the power to alter your life forever. Until that point, fear is mostly conceptual—something distant, something manageable. But when you're blindfolded, not knowing if you'll live to see another day, fear becomes very real, very fast. My experience being kidnapped by Hezbollah wasn't just a test of survival—it was a lesson in resilience, perspective, and the human capacity to endure.

The entire ordeal, from the moment we entered Dahiyeh to the moment we were released 14 hours later, unfolded like a scene from a thriller, except this wasn't fiction. It was my life. In those intense, uncertain hours, I was forced to confront deep-rooted fears and learned crucial lessons about resilience, fortitude, and finding purpose in the most unexpected places.

Resilience: The Power to Keep Going

Resilience is not built overnight. It's forged through experiences—through pain, struggle, and the moments that push you to your limits. My experience with Hezbollah wasn't my first brush with danger or fear. I've been in situations before where life seemed to hang by a thread: kidnapped once before, having a gun in my mouth, surviving a plane crash, enduring brutal bullying as a child. Each of these moments had toughened me, forcing me to adapt, to survive, and to find meaning in life's harshest lessons.

In the hours of uncertainty, waiting to see if we'd be released, killed, or imprisoned, that sense of resilience is what kept me calm. It's not that I wasn't scared—I was—but I had learned over the years that fear doesn't have to control you. Fear can sit beside you, a passenger in your mind, but it doesn't need to take the wheel. What I've learned is that resilience comes from a deep well of experience, from knowing that no matter what happens, you've survived before, and you can survive again. It's about trusting yourself to endure, to keep going, even when the path ahead is unclear.

Perspective: Shifting the Way You See the World

Perspective is everything. Throughout the ordeal, my understanding of fear and danger shifted. It's easy to think you have a handle on these things when you're in familiar environments, but throw yourself into an unknown world—a world where you have no control, no understanding of the language, and no guarantees—and perspective changes in an instant.

The most striking example of this was my wife's reaction compared to mine. While I was hyper-aware of the gravity of our situation, my wife, in her own innocent way, remained blissfully unaware of the real danger. She enjoyed her time with Hezbollah, giggling when they took her photo and relishing the food and water they offered her. Her perspective was vastly different from mine because she didn't fully grasp the stakes. And perhaps that's the lesson: the mind is capable of creating its own reality based on how it interprets the situation.

Perspective is also about understanding the world beyond your own narrow experience. I came to Lebanon knowing it was a country scarred by war, conflict, and political instability, but until I stood face to face with men who live in that world every day, it was hard to truly understand what that meant. Being in their presence, hearing their frustrations, their war stories, and their struggles gave me a deeper insight into the resilience of a people who have endured hardship beyond what many of us can imagine.

Fear: A Double-Edged Sword

Fear is primal. It's designed to protect us, to keep us alive, but it can also paralyse us. Over the course of those 14 hours, fear came and went in waves. At times, it felt like an ever-present shadow, lurking just beneath the surface of my thoughts. Other times, it was overwhelming, especially when I didn't know where my wife was, or when I had a blindfold over my eyes, unsure of where we were being taken.

But here's what I've learned about fear: it can either consume you or drive you to act. In the past, I've faced life-or-death situations, and in each of those moments, I've realised that fear is inevitable, but it's not the enemy. It's how you respond to that fear that defines the outcome. During the Hezbollah ordeal, I found that fear sharpened my senses. It made me hyper-aware of every detail, every movement, every breath. It forced me to stay calm, to think clearly, and to navigate each moment with caution.

Fear, in that sense, became a tool. It's not about being fearless—that's a myth. It's about allowing fear to exist without letting it dominate your actions. I kept my focus on what I could control: my responses, my demeanour, and my attitude. That's where fortitude comes in.

Fortitude is the ability to remain strong in the face of adversity, to stand firm when the ground beneath you is shaking. Throughout the ordeal, I had to summon an inner strength that I didn't always know I had. When I was face to face with Nasrallah, the leader of Hezbollah, I realised that my words, my actions, and my attitude would determine how things played out. This wasn't a time for weakness.

In that moment, something in me clicked. I felt a surge of defiance, not against Nasrallah or Hezbollah, but against the fear that threatened to take over. I looked him in the eye and told him the truth: I came to Lebanon because I loved the culture, the people, and the beauty of the country. I told him that, no matter what happened, I would leave with a deep appreciation for Lebanon. In that moment, I wasn't just talking to save myself—I was speaking from a place of conviction. It wasn't about bravado. It was about standing firm in my belief that life's purpose is found in these moments, where fear and strength collide.

Purpose: Finding Meaning in Adversity

Purpose is something people talk about a lot, but do they really understand it? It's easy to throw around phrases like "finding your purpose" when life is smooth, but when you're sitting in a room, being interrogated by one of the most powerful militant leaders in the world, purpose becomes much clearer.

Purpose, I've come to realise, is about making an impact even when the odds are stacked against you. It's about choosing to live authentically, even when your circumstances are extreme. During the Hezbollah ordeal, I had to think about why I was there in the first place. Was I just an adrenaline junkie who wanted a dangerous experience? Or was there something deeper? I believe I was there because I'm driven by a desire to understand the world in all its complexities—the good, the bad, and the terrifying. That's where

I find my purpose: in exploring life's extremes and using those experiences to broaden my perspective and strengthen my resilience.

In the end, it wasn't just about surviving—it was about impact. I left that room with Nasrallah knowing that I had somehow, in some small way, made an impression. I don't know if my words about loving Lebanon resonated with him, but I could see a shift in his demeanour. The same shift happened with the men who eventually apologised to us for the ordeal. They explained that they mistook us for spies, given the circumstances, but in the end, they acknowledged the mistake and made amends.

Impact isn't always about grand gestures or world-changing actions. Sometimes, it's about the small moments where you stand up for what you believe in, even in the face of fear. It's about leaving people with a sense of your integrity, your authenticity, and your willingness to face whatever comes your way.

Looking back on that experience, I realise that it fundamentally shifted the way I see the world. It taught me that resilience isn't just about surviving—it's about thriving in the face of adversity. It's about finding strength when fear threatens to overwhelm you. And it's about understanding that, no matter how dangerous or uncertain life becomes, we always have the power to choose our response.

Purpose is found in those moments where fear and fortitude intersect, where you are forced to look inward and ask yourself what truly matters. For me, it's about understanding the world, connecting with people, and leaving a positive impact, no matter how small.

And in the end, that's what life is about: resilience, perspective, and the courage to face whatever comes next.

Chapter 14

JOURNEY INTO SYRIA: A LAND OF CONTRASTS

After leaving Lebanon, our journey into Syria began with a drive from Beirut to Damascus. The landscape was rugged and hauntingly beautiful as we neared the border. Signs of recent conflict marked the road, but they were overshadowed by the vast, mountainous terrain that surrounded us. Crossing the border itself was surprisingly swift. Our fixer took care of things, exchanging some U.S. dollars for a smooth passage, and suddenly we found ourselves in Syria—a land that had long been more of a news headline than a real place to me.

Arriving in Damascus, I was struck by how alive the city felt. Despite everything Syria had endured, Damascus pulsed with life. Cafés buzzed with conversations, and people gathered on balconies and street corners. I'd expected a war-torn place, but Damascus had an energy that defied its circumstances. The old city was filled with history and beauty, and the people exuded a resilience that I couldn't help but admire.

Our guide, a young man with a nervous smile, welcomed us warmly. We were his first tour group, and his enthusiasm was contagious. He seemed excited to show us around, promising us an itinerary that would reveal Syria's hidden gems. But our trip wasn't just about Damascus; we were here to see Palmyra, the ancient city scarred by ISIS occupation and violence.

Palmyra: Beauty Amidst Ruins

The road to Palmyra took us through arid landscapes, and the journey was surreal. Palmyra, once one of the Roman Empire's greatest cities, had suffered under ISIS. As we entered the ruins, the destruction was all too evident. Ancient columns and temples lay in pieces, testaments to a once-glorious history scarred by conflict. But despite the devastation, Palmyra's beauty was undeniable. Walking through the ruins felt like a journey back in time, and I could feel the weight of its history pressing down on us.

In the tunnels ISIS had dug into the earth, I could see the haunting evidence of their occupation. But despite everything, Palmyra stood resilient. The sheer scale of the ancient city and the echo of its history were enough to remind me of the strength that can be found even in ruins.

Maaloula: A Village in the Shadow of Tragedy

That evening, our guide took us to a village called Maaloula. Nestled on a hill, this village had seen its own share of violence. ISIS had used a hotel in Maaloula as a base to carry out horrific acts against locals, and as we explored the hotel, I felt the weight of those tragedies. The walls seemed to hold memories, and at one point, we found a logbook containing the name of the last guest who had stayed there before ISIS arrived. It was a haunting reminder of the lives disrupted by war.

Standing there, I was overcome by a mix of anger, sadness, and respect for the resilience of those who had survived such horrors. Maaloula wasn't just a place of sorrow, though; it was also a symbol of resilience. The people there had faced unspeakable tragedies, yet they continued to live, love, and welcome strangers like us into their lives. That night, as we sat with the villagers, I felt a profound connection to them, as if their courage had somehow seeped into me.

Kfarbou: A Warm Welcome in a Tiny Village

Our next stop was Kfarbou, a small village with an unexpectedly vibrant spirit. We arrived to find the town decked out in Christmas lights, and though we were the only tourists there, the villagers treated us like old friends. They brought us bread and tea, gathered around us, and asked us questions with wide-eyed curiosity. For a few hours, we were part of their world, sharing laughter and stories, feeling as if we had been welcomed into a second family.

When we entered the local pub that night, we were greeted with an almost surreal experience. As we sat at a large table, every time we laughed, the entire pub seemed to laugh with us. And by the end of the evening, it felt as if the whole village had gathered in the town square to take a group photo. It was a simple act, but it held a profound meaning—the sense of community, of shared humanity, in a place so different from home. The villagers had so little to give, yet they offered it all with a warmth and generosity that left me deeply moved.

The Road to Aleppo and Meeting James

After Kfarbou, we continued towards Aleppo, passing through Hama and Homs, cities that bore the heavy scars of conflict. Entire neighbourhoods lay in ruins, reminders of lives shattered by war. But still, the people we met in those places carried on, their spirits unbroken by the devastation around them.

As we travelled, I got to know a fellow traveller, a young man I'll call James. He was slight and reserved, yet there was something about him that captured my attention. We arranged to sit together on the drive to Aleppo, and he began to share his story. At 17, James had been accepted to Harvard, and by 20, he was working in a lucrative private equity role. But the corporate life quickly wore him down. A failed relationship and the isolation of the pandemic pushed him to the brink, and in a moment of despair, he nearly took his own life. A chance encounter with Russian history sparked a fascination with Soviet culture, and eventually, the Arabic language. He quit his job, taught himself Arabic, and set off to explore the world as an English tutor, embracing the unknown, even if it meant journeying to war zones.

James's story was a reminder of resilience and the transformative power of purpose. Here was someone who had nearly lost everything, now finding meaning and connection in the most unexpected places. His courage to leave behind a life of comfort and security struck a chord in me.

Idlib: The Weight of Reality

As we neared Aleppo, we passed by Idlib, still partially under ISIS control. Missiles streaked across the sky, and I felt the reality of Syria's conflict settle over me like a heavy shroud. Our driver moved quickly, urging us not to linger. We saw sandbags along the highway, stacked as shields against stray bullets. The danger here was real, and as I watched the missiles overhead, I was struck by the contrast between this place and the safety of my home in Australia.

In that moment, I felt both lucky and humbled. Back home, we live in a bubble of comfort, often forgetting the struggles of those who live in war zones. Here, people faced danger daily, yet they carried on with a resilience and generosity that I had rarely encountered. It was a sobering reminder of how vastly different the world can be, even as we share the same earth.

Aleppo: A Deeply Personal Encounter

Arriving in Aleppo, the emotions that had simmered throughout the trip finally surfaced. Aleppo had been the inspiration for my journey to Syria, sparked by a documentary that had shown me the city's spirit, even amidst devastation. As we walked through Aleppo's markets and explored the Citadel, I was overcome with emotion. Sitting among the ruins, watching children play in the shadow of war-torn buildings, I couldn't hold back my tears.

In a small gesture, I handed out gifts to the children. One little boy accepted a gift and then hugged me tightly, and that simple act undid me. It was as though that hug symbolised everything I had felt on this journey—the love, the resilience, and the unbreakable spirit of the people here. Aleppo, with its scars and its strength, had opened my heart in ways I hadn't anticipated.

Lessons from Syria

Syria had given me more than just memories; it had taught me profound lessons. From the ancient ruins of Palmyra to the warm welcomes in Kfarbou, and the haunting reality of Maaloula, every experience had deepened my understanding of resilience and purpose. These people had endured unimaginable hardships, yet they continued to live with dignity, generosity, and an unshakeable sense of hope.

James's story reminded me that purpose is something we can find even in our darkest moments. It's about embracing life fully, stepping beyond our comfort zones, and connecting with others in meaningful ways. Syria showed me that purpose is often found not in the absence of fear, but in the courage to face it.

Moving Forward

Leaving Syria was bittersweet. The people, the land, and their stories had become a part of me, teaching me about resilience, humanity, and the power of connection. As we headed for Iraq, I carried these lessons with me, more determined than ever to live a life filled with purpose and meaning. Syria had changed me, and I knew that its people, with their unyielding spirit, would stay with me forever.

Chapter 15

THE JOURNEY INTO IRAQ — FROM CHAOS TO KINDNESS

Leaving Syria, we returned briefly to Beirut, where the trip to Iraq would begin. The Beirut airport was in chaos, with a crush of people navigating massive lines for security and immigration. The security checks weren't functioning well, creating bottlenecks that left hundreds of us waiting in the hot, crowded terminal with no water or relief in sight. People grew impatient, jumping lines and jostling for position. Somehow, after hours of pushing through the congestion, we managed to check in for our flight on Fly Baghdad, an airline under U.S. sanctions for its role in transporting military resources. We had booked the flight last-minute, as other flights were cancelled due to the war. With a mix of curiosity and trepidation, we boarded.

Fly Baghdad was unexpectedly comfortable. The crew provided us with a meal that was surprisingly delicious, and we relaxed as we flew over Syria. The sight below was an off-limits airspace, a no-fly zone typically avoided by other airlines. Despite the tension, the flight was smooth, and we arrived in Baghdad without incident. As soon as the plane landed, passengers scrambled from their seats, rushing towards the exit even as the plane was still speeding down the runway. It was both humorous and nerve-wracking, a chaotic introduction to Iraq.

Baghdad: A City of History and Resilience

In Baghdad, I was both excited and apprehensive. The city's history was legendary, yet its recent past under Saddam Hussein and subsequent conflicts cast a long shadow. Our tour guide met us and led us through bustling streets to Bucha Street, a hub for culture and commerce. We explored famous sites, took a boat cruise along the Euphrates and Tigris rivers, and admired Baghdad's historic architecture. The weight of history was tangible here; this was the heart of ancient Mesopotamia, where Civilisation first took root.

The next day, we journeyed to Babylon, a UNESCO World Heritage site and a remarkable city steeped in ancient history. Walking among its ruins, we felt transported back thousands of years, imagining the grandeur that once graced these lands. We joined a large group of tourists who welcomed us to travel with them to Saddam Hussein's grand palace. Built on a hill, it overlooked the Babylonian landscape, an imposing symbol of Saddam's vanity. Inside, I stood where his throne once sat, feeling the eerie echo of his rule. The palace was massive, and exploring its grand halls brought an unsettling mixture of awe and discomfort.

Spiritual Moments at the Shrine of Kadhimiya Shrine

Later, we visited the Kadhimiya Shrine in Baghdad, a significant site for Shia Muslims. The experience was both overwhelming and humbling. Men and women entered separate sections of the shrine, and the energy was intense. My wife, who was with the women, later told me of the powerful spiritual atmosphere she had felt. The shrine was filled with prayers and reverence, and though I wasn't part of this faith, the profound dedication and holiness of the place left a deep impression on me.

Hatra and Mosul: The Beauty and Brutality of History

After exploring Baghdad, we travelled to Hatra, a breathtaking UNESCO site, where remnants of ancient walls and temples bore witness to Iraq's rich cultural heritage. Hatra had once been an ISIS stronghold, and scars from that occupation were still visible. Bullet holes marked walls where ISIS fighters had practised shooting, and damage from the conflict was stark. Meeting the local manager, who had lived in fear of ISIS for nearly two years, deepened my respect for the resilience of the Iraqi people. He described hiding in his home, wondering when ISIS might knock on his door. Hatra was both beautiful and tragic, a place where history and horror coexisted.

Our journey continued to Mosul, a city that had endured unimaginable suffering under ISIS occupation. We visited the mosque where ISIS leader Abu Bakr al-Baghdadi had declared his caliphate before destroying the mosque when defeat seemed imminent. The rubble of the mosque was a somber reminder of the horrors the city had witnessed. Walking through Mosul's streets, I encountered a neighbourhood recently rebuilt with vibrant pink and blue walls—a hopeful effort to restore normalcy amid the ruins.

It was here that I met an elderly tailor whose story left an indelible mark on me. He and his family had suffered immensely under ISIS. His three sons had been executed, his wife was taken by ISIS leaders and later killed, and yet here he was, offering us warmth and generosity. As he shared his story, his resilience and grace in the face of such loss left me speechless. He invited us into his shop, fed us, and even smiled for a photo with my wife. In that moment, I felt both heartbreak and profound admiration. This man had lost nearly everything, yet he chose kindness.

Reflections on Humanity and Resilience

Meeting the tailor in Mosul was one of the most moving experiences of my life. As I took a photo of him, I was overwhelmed by a rush of conflicting thoughts—gratitude for my own life, grief for his loss, and frustration at the injustices people like him had endured. In the face of unspeakable tragedy, he had chosen to be gracious, offering strangers kindness when many would have chosen bitterness. It made me reflect on the corporate world I had left behind, on the people who wielded their power with arrogance rather than empathy. This tailor's quiet strength and resilience were a stark contrast to the pettiness and cruelty I had witnessed in my former career.

Chapter 16

IRAQI KURDISTAN: CONNECTION AMIDST TRANQUILITY

Our journey continued into Iraqi Kurdistan, where we joined a tour group in Erbil. Compared to other parts of Iraq, Kurdistan felt more peaceful, almost serene. We visited cultural landmarks like Lalish, a holy site for the Yazidi people, and even witnessed a baptism, an intimate and beautiful ritual that felt like a celebration of life amidst so much hardship.

In Erbil, we met an old friend who had been among the first to congratulate my wife and me when we got engaged years earlier. Reuniting with him after nearly a decade was a poignant reminder of the connections that transcend borders and time. Both times we met for dinner, we ended up at an Indian restaurant, a comforting taste of home after weeks of kebabs and falafel.

As we prepared to leave Kurdistan, we received unsettling news: a nearby U.S. military base had been hit by a drone strike. Our flight was parked adjacent to the base, but fortunately, we were able to board safely and begin the long journey back to Australia.

Leaving Iraq, I felt a complex mixture of relief, gratitude, and sorrow. This journey had challenged me to see beyond my own comfortable world and to appreciate the strength and humanity of those who endure hardship daily. Iraq had shown me both beauty and brutality, resilience and despair. It left me with a renewed understanding of the human spirit and the importance of kindness and empathy, even in the darkest of times. The stories of the people I met, from the tailor in Mosul to the villagers in Kfarbou, would stay with me forever, shaping my understanding of purpose and resilience in ways I hadn't thought possible.

Chapter 17

AFTER THE TRIP: CHANGED PERSPECTIVES

The experience in Lebanon left an indelible mark on me—a blend of fear, survival, and the unexpected kindness of strangers in the heart of a place known more for its tension than its warmth. Reflecting on this and the months that followed, I found myself questioning the concept of purpose in a way that I hadn't before. Purpose isn't just a neatly defined goal we aim for; rather, it's something that emerges through life's most unexpected trials. Our time in the Middle East opened our eyes to how closely connected purpose, resilience, and understanding are.

In each interaction, from the small kindnesses of strangers offering bread in Lebanon's markets to the more harrowing moments in Hezbollah's stronghold, I began to see life from a different vantage point. The depth of my feelings during this trip made me realise that purpose can't always be found within the safety of routine; sometimes, it is born in the face of fear, when we confront situations that strip away our comfort and test our character.

Reflecting on what I had seen and experienced, I found a new sense of gratitude. Lebanon's people, despite a complex political reality and limited resources, were generous in spirit and unwavering in their resilience. Strangers greeted us, sharing what little they had, and they laughed with us in the markets despite everything. These moments, I realised, were filled with purpose too—simple, powerful exchanges that reminded me of the importance of resilience and unity. In places like these, where people have little to give, the act of sharing itself is profound.

In our modern lives, we sometimes lose sight of purpose, becoming absorbed in work, material comfort, and achievements. We may find ourselves aiming for impact or success, but what does it mean to truly live with purpose? I used to think purpose was something tied to accomplishments, titles, or financial success. But purpose, I learned, was not a destination I could reach. Instead, it was an experience—a continuous process shaped by the people we meet and the ways we choose to respond to life's unexpected challenges. This was especially clear during my encounter with Nasrallah, a moment where fear and fortitude collided.

Looking back, I can see that purpose was in the choice to show respect, humility, and honesty in a situation where my life was no longer in my control. Purpose is also in the courage to admit to oneself that the corporate path I had chosen was no longer serving me, that it was time to step into the unknown and find something truer to who I am. The Lebanon experience crystallised these reflections, reinforcing that purpose is found not in comfort but in the uncharted.

This journey also taught me about resilience in its purest form. Resilience is about standing firm when the ground beneath you shifts, when every instinct tells you to retreat. In those tense hours under Hezbollah's scrutiny, my resolve was tested as never before, and I realised that resilience isn't only about facing fear—it's about finding a way to hold on to what you value most, even in the face of fear.

The Middle East journey sparked a deeper introspection, challenging me to confront aspects of myself and of life that I had overlooked. It reminded me that we are all connected by shared humanity, that kindness and resilience can thrive in the least likely of places. These were lessons I could not have found anywhere else. I left Lebanon not only with stories of beauty, resilience, and fortitude but with a renewed understanding of what it means to live a purposeful life—a life rooted in integrity, compassion, and an unyielding drive to seek meaning.

For me, the Middle East adventure was about more than the destinations; it was about connecting with the people, the land, and its complex history. And it became a way to challenge my own assumptions about what matters in life. As I continue my journey, I am more certain that true purpose lies in resilience, in facing the unknown, and in making the choice to grow. I hope that by sharing this story, others may be inspired to look beyond the surface, to search for the meaning that calls to them, and to never shy away from the paths that seem difficult or unknown.

Part 3
THE PROFESSIONAL PIVOT

Chapter 18

THE CORPORATE WORLD: SUCCESS AND STAGNATION

The Corporate World: Success and Stagnation

For over 20 years, my career unfolded within the corporate world—a journey that, while unintended, came to define a significant chapter of my life. I never actively chose this path; in many ways, it chose me. My original trajectory pointed in a completely different direction, towards professional tennis, a career I had passionately pursued in my youth. Tennis, too, had felt like it had chosen me, a serendipitous alignment of skill, opportunity, and dedication. Yet life has a way of steering us into the unexpected, and when I found myself stepping away from tennis, the corporate world became the next arena where I could test my limits, refine my skills, and challenge myself.

I approached this world with the same determination I had brought to tennis, but it didn't take long to see that the playing field was different. Working across diverse sectors—consulting, healthcare, resources, and sustainability—I experienced both the exhilarating highs of professional success and the disheartening lows that come with navigating toxic environments.

In the early years, consulting became a formative experience. I was fortunate to work alongside emotionally intelligent mentors who inspired me, not just with their technical expertise but with their ability to lead with empathy and integrity. Under their guidance, I believed the corporate world was a place where I could thrive. These were individuals who valued collaboration, encouraged creativity, and saw their team members as people, not just resources.

However, as I transitioned into in-house corporate roles, a different reality began to emerge. The culture, once aspirational, started to reveal a less savoury side. I witnessed dismissive attitudes, unethical practices, and a pervasive undercurrent of ego and power struggles. These behaviours weren't isolated to one role or one organisation—they seemed embedded within the system itself. While I still encountered remarkable individuals who upheld strong values, they were often the exception rather than the rule.

The Pandemic Shift: Entrepreneurship

The global pandemic in 2020 marked a turning point, both personally and professionally. Like many others, I faced sudden upheaval when I lost my job. At first, this disruption felt like a setback, but it quickly became an opportunity—a chance to step back, reassess, and chart a new course.

For four months, I ventured into entrepreneurship. It was a liberating experience, one that revealed the depth of my own potential and the scope of the impact I could make when freed from the constraints of corporate hierarchies. I discovered a renewed sense of purpose in this work, crafting solutions that directly aligned with my values and seeing the tangible effects of my efforts.

Yet, even as I began to find my footing in this new space, there was a lingering sense that my professional journey wasn't quite complete. I felt the need to "round out" my corporate experience—to polish my skillset and gain deeper insights into areas like ESG (Environmental, Social, and Governance) and sustainability. When an opportunity arose in Sydney, I embraced it, drawn by the promise of growth and the chance to contribute to meaningful change in an area I cared deeply about.

This role came with an attractive financial package, but money had never been my primary motivator. For me, success had always been about impact—about using my skills to create value and foster positive change. Initially, the position seemed like a perfect fit, offering both professional challenges and personal alignment.

But it didn't take long for cracks to appear. The culture around me was misaligned with my values. While I was learning and expanding my professional toolkit, I was also grappling with an environment that felt increasingly toxic. Arrogance, dismissiveness, and a disregard for dignity permeated the workplace. These behaviours weren't confined to management; they trickled down through teams, creating a pervasive sense of negativity.

Despite these challenges, there were bright spots—individuals who stood out for their kindness, intelligence, and professionalism. These people reminded me that even in the most difficult environments, there is always potential for connection and inspiration. Yet, their presence wasn't enough to offset the broader issues.

2024: A Pivotal Year

In 2024, I made another move, this time to Melbourne, in the hopes of finding a role that aligned more closely with my values and aspirations. But once again, I encountered the same systemic issues that had begun to define my corporate experience. This time, however, the disconnect felt even more personal.

One particularly jarring moment came during a board presentation. Earlier in the day, I had done a dry run with my manager, who proceeded to critique my character and work quality in a manner that, while not overtly hostile, was deeply condescending and belittling. The experience left me questioning my value and the purpose of my contributions.

Hours later, when I presented to the board, my strategy was not only accepted but endorsed. This validation was bittersweet. While it confirmed the quality of my work, it also underscored the disconnect between my contributions and the respect I received within the organisation. The moment crystallised a growing realisation: my time in the corporate world had run its course.

Chapter 19
CONFRONTING THE QUESTION OF PURPOSE

In the aftermath of this experience, I sought clarity. I travelled to India to visit my father, who was unwell at the time, and posed a question that had been weighing on my mind: "Is it me? Am I the problem? Am I too soft, too idealistic for the corporate world?" His response was both affirming and challenging. "It's not you," he said, "but it is you. You know what you need to do—you've always known."

Returning to Melbourne, I took this advice to heart. I consulted my closest circle of trust, ten individuals whose perspectives I deeply valued. I asked them a simple but profound question: "Should I go left or right?" Their unanimous response was clear: it was time to go right, to leave the corporate world behind and pursue a path that truly aligned with my values.

With the support of my wife, who encouraged me despite the risks of leaving behind a stable income, I made the decision to quit. It was a leap of faith into the unknown, but it was also a step towards living with greater authenticity and purpose.

Lessons from the Corporate World

Looking back, my time in the corporate world was a journey of contrasts. It was filled with moments of triumph and learning, as well as instances of disillusionment and frustration. But through it all, it shaped me in profound ways.

I learned that success is not solely about climbing the ladder or accumulating accolades; it's about finding meaning in the work you do and aligning it with your values. I saw firsthand how leadership—both good and bad—can profoundly impact not only an organisation's outcomes but also the well-being of its people.

I also came to understand that culture is everything. The most skilled teams and ambitious strategies can be derailed by a toxic environment, just as the simplest initiatives can thrive in a culture of trust and respect.

Finally, I learned the importance of self-awareness. The corporate world tested my resilience, challenged my values, and ultimately led me to confront a fundamental question: What kind of life do I want to live? The answer, I realised, lay not in adapting to a system that didn't align with my values but in creating a path where I could live and work with integrity.

A New Chapter

Leaving the corporate world was not an easy decision, but it was the right one. It marked the beginning of a new chapter, one defined by a commitment to purpose, impact, and authenticity.

This transition wasn't without its challenges. There were moments of doubt, times when I questioned whether I had made the right choice. But each time, I returned to the lessons I had learned from my journey—the importance of resilience, the power of values-driven work, and the strength that comes from living authentically.

As I moved forward, I carried with me the insights and experiences that had shaped me. The corporate world, with all its successes and shortcomings, had prepared me for this next phase, equipping me with the tools to navigate uncertainty and embrace the possibilities of the unknown.

Today, I work not for a title or a paycheck but for a purpose that resonates deeply with who I am. My professional pivot has been a journey of rediscovery—of returning to what truly matters and building a life that reflects my values and aspirations. It is a journey that, while far from complete, fills me with gratitude and hope for what lies ahead.

Chapter 20

THE LEAP OF FAITH

By February 2024, I had reached a critical juncture in my professional life. The corporate world, which had once been a stage for learning, growth, and achievement, now felt constricting, even toxic. The experiences that had shaped me—both the triumphs and the disillusionments—seemed to point in one direction: it was time to leave.

This decision didn't come lightly. I sought clarity and wisdom, starting with my father during a trip to India. He was unwell at the time, but his advice cut through the fog of uncertainty that had clouded my mind. I asked him, "Is it just me? Am I too soft, too nice? Am I the problem?" He responded with a mix of candour and encouragement: "It's not you, but it is you. You have the skills, the experience, and the knowledge to make a real impact—don't waste that by staying with people who don't align with your values." His words were a revelation, affirming what I already suspected deep down: I had outgrown the corporate world.

Returning to Melbourne, I turned to my trusted circle of advisors—friends, colleagues, and mentors who knew me well and whose opinions I valued deeply. I presented them with a simple but daunting question: "What should I do next?" Almost unanimously, they encouraged me to take a new path, one that was more aligned with my values and aspirations.

The next conversation was with my wife, whose unwavering support had been a constant throughout my career. I was acutely aware that this decision wouldn't just impact me—it would affect our household, our financial stability, and our shared future. I asked her, "If I can make enough to keep food on the table, pay the bills, and allow us to travel once or twice a year, would that be enough?" She hesitated, understandably cautious about the uncertainties ahead. But ultimately, her faith in me outweighed her fears. Her belief became my anchor as I prepared to take the leap.

With the encouragement of my father, the guidance of my inner circle, and the support of my wife, I made the decision. In February 2024, I quit my corporate job. There was no safety net, no pre-existing business waiting to catch me. The path ahead was uncharted, but for the first time in years, I felt a sense of alignment between my values and my direction.

Defining Purpose on My Own Terms

Stepping away from the corporate world wasn't just about leaving behind a job—it was about redefining success and purpose. I had spent years in environments where success was measured by titles, bonuses, and bottom-line achievements. But these metrics no longer resonated with me.

As I pondered my next steps, I began to reflect on what I truly loved and what gave me a sense of fulfillment. I thought about the moments in my career that had brought me joy: mentoring young professionals, teaching concepts that inspired others, delivering impactful public speeches, and consulting on sustainability projects that aligned with my values. These were the activities that energised me, that made me feel I was contributing something meaningful to the world.

Slowly, the pieces of a new venture began to take shape. I

envisioned a business built on four core pillars: **teaching, coaching, consulting,** and **public speaking**. Each pillar reflected a passion of mine and offered a way to create impact beyond the confines of a traditional corporate role. My work would be about more than profit—it would be about helping people grow, fostering resilience, and guiding others to align their actions with their values.

The Birth of Orka Advisory

Choosing a name for this new venture was an important step. I wanted something that encapsulated the ethos of what I was building—an organisation that emphasised action, integrity, and resilience. My search led me to a Swedish word: **"Orka."**

Orka translates roughly to "the will to get things done," a phrase that resonated deeply with me. It reflected my own approach to life and work, an attitude of perseverance and determination. Additionally, in its colloquial usage, Orka carries an edge of defiance, an unwillingness to tolerate nonsense. It was perfect.

With the name in place, **Orka Advisory** was born. But unlike most businesses, Orka didn't start with a detailed business plan or a meticulously crafted marketing strategy. I didn't have a roadmap or a five-year projection. Instead, I relied on my instincts, my values, and the lessons I'd learned from years of navigating complex professional landscapes.

My mission for Orka was ambitious yet simple: **to positively impact 20,000 people within the first year.** This wasn't just a private goal; it was one I shared publicly on LinkedIn, a way of holding myself accountable and demonstrating that my focus was on people, not profits. For the first time, my measure of success wasn't tied to financial metrics—it was tied to the lives I could touch, the transformations I could help facilitate.

Challenges and Growth

The months following my decision to quit were both exhilarating and challenging. Starting from scratch meant embracing uncertainty in ways I hadn't before. There were days when doubt crept in, when I questioned whether I had made the right choice. Was this path sustainable? Would Orka Advisory resonate with the people I hoped to serve?

Yet, even in these moments of doubt, I found strength in the sense of purpose that had driven my decision. I thought back to my experiences in the Middle East, to the people I had met in Lebanon, Syria, and Iraq. They had shown me what resilience looked like in its purest form—facing unimaginable adversity with strength, kindness, and an unwavering sense of purpose. If they could endure and thrive in such circumstances, surely I could navigate the uncertainties of entrepreneurship.

Every milestone, no matter how small, became a reminder of why I had chosen this path. The first coaching session, the first workshop, the first speaking engagement—all of these moments reinforced my belief in the mission of Orka Advisory. I wasn't just building a business; I was building a platform for impact, a space where I could help others discover their potential and align their actions with their values.

Purpose Beyond Profit

One of the most liberating aspects of this journey has been the ability to redefine success on my own terms. In the corporate world, success often felt like an external construct—something dictated by organisational goals and societal expectations. Now, success is deeply personal.

For me, success isn't about revenue or recognition. It's about the stories of the people I've been able to help. It's about the professional who found clarity and confidence through coaching, the team that left a workshop feeling inspired and empowered, the young leader who discovered their voice through mentorship. Each of these stories is a testament to the power of purpose-driven work.

Through Orka, I've also discovered the joy of freedom—freedom to choose the projects I take on, the clients I work with, and the values I uphold. This freedom has allowed me to stay true to my principles, to prioritise integrity over convenience, and to focus on impact over profit.

Lessons from the Journey

The journey of starting Orka Advisory has been one of profound learning and growth. Among the most important lessons I've learned are:

1. **Resilience is Key:** Stepping into the unknown requires a deep well of resilience. There will be setbacks, doubts, and challenges, but resilience allows you to navigate these with grace and determination.
2. **Purpose is a Journey, Not a Destination:** Finding purpose isn't about arriving at a single, definitive answer. It's about continuously aligning your actions with your values and staying open to growth and change.
3. **Impact Outweighs Profit:** True fulfillment comes from the difference you make in the lives of others. When you focus on impact, success naturally follows.
4. **Trust Your Instincts:** In the absence of a roadmap, your instincts become your guide. Trusting yourself and your vision is essential when building something new.

A Circle of Trust: The Role of My Mother in Believing in Me

When I first contemplated leaving the corporate world, I knew the decision wouldn't be easy. I wasn't just stepping away from a stable career—I was stepping into uncertainty. The prospect was both liberating and terrifying, and I needed clarity. To find it, I turned to the people I trusted the most.

I consulted ten people—friends, mentors, former colleagues, and family members—each of whom had played a significant role in shaping my life and career. These were people whose opinions I deeply valued, whose perspectives I trusted, and whose support I knew would be unwavering. Their responses were overwhelmingly positive. They told me I had the skills, experience, and values to succeed on my own. They urged me to take the leap, reminding me of the strength I had shown in other moments of transition and growth.

Yet, even with their encouragement, the weight of the decision lingered. There's something uniquely daunting about choosing a path that feels right in your heart but goes against conventional wisdom. The logical part of me worried about financial stability, the potential for failure, and the implications of this decision on my family. I needed one voice to rise above the others, a voice that could cut through the noise of doubt and indecision.

That voice belonged to my mother.

A Lifetime of Belief

My mother has always been my fiercest supporter. Throughout my life, she has been a source of unconditional love and unwavering belief, even when I doubted myself. She saw potential in me before I saw it in myself and pushed me to aim higher, dream bigger, and stay true to my values.

When I shared my plan with her, she didn't hesitate. "You've always known what you need to do," she said. "You just have to believe in yourself as much as I believe in you." Her words were simple, but they carried the weight of years of encouragement, faith, and a deep understanding of who I was at my core.

Unlike some of the others I consulted, my mother didn't need to analyse the risks or weigh the pros and cons. Her belief in me wasn't based on spreadsheets or logic—it was based on knowing me, deeply and intimately, in a way that only a parent can. She trusted my instincts and my abilities, even when I wasn't sure if I could trust them myself.

The Power of Her Belief

What made my mother's belief so powerful was the history behind it. She had seen me navigate life's challenges, from the highs of professional success to the lows of personal setbacks. She knew how hard I had worked, how much I had learned, and how deeply I cared about making a meaningful impact.

But it wasn't just my achievements that fueled her confidence in me—it was my values. She often told me, "Your values are your greatest strength. They guide you, and they'll guide others too." My mother believed that my commitment to integrity, compassion, and purpose would be the foundation of whatever I chose to build next.

Her words became a mantra for me in those early days of uncertainty. Whenever doubt crept in, I reminded myself of her unwavering faith. It was as though she had given me permission to trust myself, to lean into my instincts, and to embrace the unknown with courage.

More Than Encouragement: A Call to Action

My mother's belief in me wasn't just about cheering me on from the sidelines. It was a call to action. She challenged me to rise to the occasion, to prove to myself that I was capable of more than I had ever imagined. Her faith was a reminder that I wasn't just stepping away from something—I was stepping towards something bigger, something better.

Her encouragement also carried an emotional weight that grounded me. While others focused on the external aspects of my decision—what I would do, how I would make money, or how I would manage the risks—my mother focused on the internal journey. "This is about who you are, not just what you do," she told me. "And who you are is enough."

Balancing Support and Skepticism

While my mother was my strongest supporter, she wasn't naive about the challenges ahead. She understood that starting a business was a significant risk, especially when leaving the security of a corporate career. But rather than let those risks define the conversation, she reframed them as opportunities. "Every challenge is a chance to learn," she said. "You've overcome obstacles before, and you'll overcome these too."

Her perspective helped me see the journey not as a leap into the abyss but as a step forward into growth and possibility. She reminded me that failure wasn't something to fear—it was something to embrace as part of the process.

A Legacy of Resilience

My mother's belief in me wasn't just about this one decision—it was part of a lifelong legacy of resilience and support. Growing up, I had watched her face her own challenges with grace and determination. She had taught me what it meant to persevere, to stay true to one's values, and to find strength in the face of adversity.

Her example became a guiding light for me as I navigated the uncertainty of leaving the corporate world. I often thought about her ability to find meaning and purpose, even in difficult circumstances. It was a reminder that purpose isn't about avoiding challenges—it's about finding strength within them.

The Impact of One Voice

In the end, it was my mother's voice that tipped the scales. The ten people I consulted gave me invaluable advice, encouragement, and perspective. But it was her belief that gave me the courage to act. She reminded me that I wasn't just capable of success—I was capable of creating something meaningful, something that aligned with who I truly was.

Her words have stayed with me throughout this journey. They echo in my mind during moments of doubt, reassuring me that I made the right decision. They remind me that I am not alone, that I carry her faith with me in everything I do.

As I continue to build Orka Advisory, I often think about the role my mother played in shaping this journey. Her belief in me wasn't just a gift—it was a responsibility, a call to live up to the potential she saw in me. And for that, I am endlessly grateful.

Her faith has become the foundation of my own belief in myself, a reminder that even in the face of uncertainty, I am capable of great things. And in every client I coach, every team I consult, and every audience I speak to, I hope to pass on a little of the confidence and encouragement that my mother so generously gave to me.

Looking Ahead

As Orka Advisory continues to grow, I'm filled with gratitude for the journey so far. Each day brings new opportunities to learn, to connect, and to make a difference. The path I've chosen is far from conventional, but it is one that feels deeply aligned with who I am and what I value.

Looking ahead, my vision for Orka is to expand its reach and deepen its impact. I want to continue fostering growth, resilience, and purpose in others, helping individuals and organisations alike navigate their own pivots and transformations.

The decision to leave the corporate world was a leap of faith, but it was also a leap towards authenticity. It marked the beginning of a new chapter—one defined not by external expectations but by a commitment to living and working in alignment with my values.

Through Orka Advisory, I'm not just building a business; I'm building a legacy. A legacy of integrity, impact, and resilience—a testament to the power of purpose and the courage to pursue it.

Part 4
FINDING MEANING IN LIFE'S JOURNEY

Chapter 21
THE INTERSECTION OF TRAVEL AND PURPOSE

Travel is often seen as an escape—a chance to step outside the routines of daily life and experience the world anew. For me, however, travel has always been far more profound. It is a lens through which I have come to understand not just the world but myself, a practice of self-exploration as much as global discovery. It is an unending journey, one that has profoundly shaped my understanding of purpose and life's deeper meanings. Immersing myself in unfamiliar places has taught me a guiding principle: purpose, much like travel, is not about a fixed endpoint. Instead, it's an evolving understanding, shaped by every encounter, lesson, and risk along the way.

In my early years as a traveller, the appeal lay in the thrill of adventure and the allure of foreign landscapes. But as time went on, and I found myself in more complex and challenging environments, I began to see travel as something deeper. It wasn't just about visiting new places but about expanding my boundaries, confronting the unknown, and discovering parts of myself I hadn't yet encountered. Each journey became a step in an unfolding path towards understanding purpose—not as a destination but as a constantly evolving way of being.

The Transformative Power of Encounters

When I reflect on my travels, the encounters I've had with people stand out as defining moments. Each interaction felt like a microcosm of the human experience—a brief but powerful reminder of our shared struggles, hopes, fears, and resilience. The stories of the people I met, often filled with hardship and loss, revealed a capacity for generosity and strength that left an indelible mark on me.

In Lebanon, for example, I met a shopkeeper in Beirut. An elderly man who had lived through decades of instability, he welcomed me into his small shop with a warmth that felt almost otherworldly given the struggles he had endured. He offered me sweets and shared stories of rebuilding his life after every setback, proudly pointing to photographs lining the walls—snapshots of family, friends, and milestones. Despite having little material wealth, he exuded a richness of spirit that was humbling. From him, I learned that purpose doesn't require grand achievements. It can be found in the simple act of carrying on with grace, extending kindness, and finding joy in small moments.

Syria, by contrast, confronted me with resilience on a different scale. I arrived in Damascus filled with curiosity but also apprehension. The narratives I'd absorbed about the region painted a picture of despair, but what I encountered was something far more nuanced. In the bustling markets of Aleppo, amid the ruins of a city once celebrated for its vibrancy, I saw traces of sorrow etched into the landscape. Yet, woven into the fabric of everyday life was also an unmistakable sense of perseverance. People greeted me with smiles, their hospitality unshaken despite years of war. Watching them rebuild their lives one brick at a time, I learned that purpose can be as simple and profound as maintaining hope in the face of unimaginable devastation.

These encounters underscored an important truth: life's purpose often reveals itself not in moments of triumph but in quiet acts of endurance and connection. The tailor in Mosul who invited me into his shop, the children in Iraq who turned a dusty street into a playground, the women in Syria who cooked meals amid the rubble—these people taught me that purpose is rooted in our ability to find meaning in the everyday and to connect with others through shared humanity.

> **Lesson:** Purpose is shaped in the presence of others, through moments of shared humanity that remind us of the strength in compassion and connection.

Resilience and Purpose in Adversity

One of the most transformative aspects of travel is how it reveals the resilience of the human spirit, especially in places where adversity is a part of daily life. In my journeys, I witnessed countless examples of people who faced hardship with courage, finding ways to rise above circumstances that would overwhelm most.

In Iraq, I visited villages where bullet-ridden walls bore silent witness to years of conflict. Yet, within these same villages, I saw families laughing together, children playing, and communities working to rebuild. In Mosul, a tailor who had lost his family to war spoke to me with a quiet dignity that I found both humbling and inspiring. He shared his story, showed me a photo of his children, and offered me tea—an act of generosity that seemed almost surreal given the weight of his loss. Through his example, I began to understand that resilience is not just about surviving; it's about choosing hope over despair and finding purpose in the face of hardship.

The resilience I witnessed in these places was a profound reminder that purpose is often born from adversity. It isn't about waiting for perfect conditions but about finding strength in imperfection, joy in small victories, and meaning in the act of persevering.

> **Lesson:** Resilience is not just enduring hardship but choosing to rise above it, finding purpose even when the path is uncertain.

The Role of Vulnerability in Transformation

Travel pushes us into unfamiliar territory, not just geographically but emotionally and mentally. It requires vulnerability—an openness to being wrong, to being humbled, and to confronting our limitations. In this vulnerability lies the potential for transformation.

There were moments during my travels when I felt utterly exposed, whether it was navigating a language I didn't understand or confronting the stark realities of life in a conflict zone. These experiences stripped away the illusion of control and forced me to rely on trust—both in myself and in the kindness of strangers. I came to see vulnerability not as a weakness but as a doorway to growth.

In Lebanon, I experienced this vulnerability firsthand during an encounter with a group of locals who initially viewed me with suspicion. As tensions eased, our conversations turned to shared experiences and mutual understanding. By the end of the evening, we were sharing stories and laughing together, our differences eclipsed by the bonds we had formed. Moments like this taught me that vulnerability allows us to connect on a deeper level, breaking down barriers and revealing our shared humanity.

> **Lesson:** Vulnerability is not a weakness; it is a strength that fosters connection, understanding, and personal growth.

Purpose as an Evolving Journey

Perhaps the most profound lesson I've learned from travel is that purpose, like life itself, is not static. It is not a destination we arrive at but a journey we undertake, one shaped by the places we go, the people we meet, and the experiences we embrace. Each trip, each encounter, adds a layer to our understanding of purpose, creating a mosaic that is as dynamic and multifaceted as the world itself.

This realisation has been both liberating and humbling. It has freed me from the pressure to define purpose in rigid terms, allowing me instead to embrace its fluidity. In every new place, I find new insights—whether it's the strength of a community rebuilding after war, the joy of a shared meal in a bustling market, or the wisdom of an elder passing down stories. Purpose, I've come to see, is not about achieving a single goal but about living in alignment with our values and making a positive impact wherever we can.

> **Lesson:** Purpose is a journey, not a destination. It evolves with each experience, shaped by our willingness to learn, grow, and connect.

What I Hope Readers Take Away

Through my travels, I've come to believe that purpose is not something we find; it's something we create. It's an evolving understanding shaped by the choices we make, the connections we form, and the values we uphold. For those seeking purpose, I would offer this: embrace the journey. Allow yourself to be curious, to take risks, and to venture beyond the boundaries of what is familiar.

Travel has taught me that life's most profound lessons often come from unexpected places—from the kindness of a stranger, the resilience of a community, or the beauty of a shared moment. It has shown me that purpose is not a grand achievement but a collection of small, meaningful actions that ripple outward, creating positive change in ways we may never fully see.

My hope is that readers will see travel not as an escape but as an invitation—to step outside their comfort zones, to embrace vulnerability, and to discover the depth of their own potential. In doing so, I believe they will find not just the world's beauty but their own unique place within it.

> **Lesson:** Purpose is not found in what we accomplish but in how we live—in the connections we make, the values we uphold, and the courage we show in embracing life's journey.

Travel has been my greatest teacher, revealing truths about resilience, compassion, and the infinite potential of the human spirit. It has shown me that the journey towards purpose is as important as the purpose itself—a journey of continuous discovery, growth, and connection. And it is a journey I hope to continue for the rest of my life.

Travel is often seen as an escape—a chance to step outside the routines of daily life and experience the world anew. For me, however, travel has always been far more profound. It is a lens through which I have come to understand not just the world but myself, a practice of self-exploration as much as global discovery. It is an unending journey, one that has profoundly shaped my understanding of purpose and life's deeper meanings. Immersing myself in unfamiliar places has taught me a guiding principle: purpose, much like travel, is not about a fixed endpoint. Instead, it's an evolving understanding, shaped by every encounter, lesson, and risk along the way.

In my early years as a traveller, the appeal lay in the thrill of adventure and the allure of foreign landscapes. But as time went on, and I found myself in more complex and challenging environments, I began to see travel as something deeper. It wasn't just about visiting new places but about expanding my boundaries, confronting the unknown, and discovering parts of myself I hadn't yet encountered. Each journey became a step in an unfolding path toward understanding purpose—not as a destination but as a constantly evolving way of being.

Self-Discovery on the Road

Travel is a catalyst for self-discovery because it compels us to face ourselves in ways we might never encounter in the familiarity of routine. It strips away the comfort of the known and pushes us into unfamiliar environments where our habits, tendencies, and assumptions are challenged. The disorientation of navigating a foreign language, the vulnerability of being a stranger in a new culture, and the unpredictability of unfamiliar situations force us to confront who we are at our core.

For me, travel has always been a mirror reflecting my truest self, with all its strengths and flaws laid bare. Through my journeys, I began to see my adaptability, curiosity, and resilience more clearly. But travel also illuminated my weaknesses—my impatience, my occasional need for control, and my tendency to rush through experiences instead of savouring them. These revelations weren't always comfortable, but they were necessary for growth.

In the bustling markets of Nigeria, I learned patience as I navigated the chaos of vendors haggling and customers jostling for space. In India, I was reminded of the beauty of slowing down, as locals invited me to sit, sip chai, and share stories without the constant rush of modern life. But it was in places like Iraq, where tension and uncertainty were part of daily life, that I learned the most transformative lesson: to let go of control and embrace trust.

In Iraq, I found myself in situations where planning and strategy had little value. Walking through the war-scarred streets of Mosul, uncertainty was the only certainty. Yet, in those moments, I discovered an inner calm I didn't know I had—the ability to trust in myself, in the kindness of strangers, and in the unfolding of events beyond my control. I realised that resilience doesn't come from clinging to plans but from adapting to change and finding strength in vulnerability.

Lesson: Purpose is not a rigid plan; it's an openness to life's unpredictability and a willingness to grow through it.

Embracing Hardship and Growth

There were times, of course, when I questioned my attraction to challenging destinations. Why was I drawn to places where risks were real, comforts were few, and the path was far from easy? Yet, each time I returned from these journeys, I felt an undeniable shift in my perspective. Hardship, I found, was not something to avoid but something to embrace. It was in the face of adversity that I discovered the depths of my own strength and the resilience of others.

In Syria, I met families living among the ruins of cities once vibrant with life. Their daily existence was a testament to endurance, their smiles a defiance of despair. They didn't have the luxury of choosing their circumstances, but they chose hope and perseverance. Witnessing their resilience taught me that purpose is not found in avoiding hardship but in rising above it.

Each challenge I faced on the road—whether navigating cultural misunderstandings, adapting to unpredictable conditions, or confronting my own fears—became an opportunity for growth. I began to see every setback as a stepping stone and every moment of discomfort as a chance to learn. This mindset didn't just transform my travels; it transformed how I approached life as a whole.

Lesson: Hardship is not an obstacle but a pathway to growth and self-discovery.

The Legacy of Connection

One of the most profound lessons I've learned through travel is that purpose often lies in connection. It's not about the places we visit but the people we meet and the relationships we form along the way. These connections have the power to shape us, to teach us, and to leave an indelible mark on our journey.

In Mosul, I met a tailor whose life had been shattered by war. He had lost his family, his home, and nearly everything he held dear. Yet, he greeted me with kindness, inviting me into his shop, sharing his story, and even offering me food. His quiet dignity and generosity in the face of unimaginable loss were humbling. He didn't speak of bitterness or revenge; instead, he showed me the strength of a heart that chooses compassion over despair.

That encounter stayed with me long after I left Iraq. It reminded me of the vast capacity for kindness within people, even when life strips them of almost everything. The tailor's resilience became a lesson in purpose—not the kind of purpose driven by ambition or achievement, but one rooted in connection and humanity.

> **Lesson:** True purpose is found in how we connect with others, how we uplift them, and how we choose to respond to life's hardships with kindness.

Carrying Stories as Gifts

Every journey I've taken has left me with stories—stories of people whose lives have touched mine in ways both profound and subtle. These stories have become part of who I am, shaping my worldview and guiding my actions. They are gifts that remind me of the beauty and complexity of the human experience.

In Lebanon, I was struck by the warmth and resilience of a community rebuilding itself after years of conflict. In Kurdistan, I met Yazidi families who had survived unimaginable atrocities but continued to preserve their culture and traditions with quiet strength. Each story added a new layer to my understanding of humanity, teaching me that resilience is not just an individual trait but a collective one.

Travelling through these places taught me to value storytelling as a means of connection and growth. Each person I met carried a unique narrative, and each narrative held lessons that I could carry forward. The stories I encountered weren't just about survival; they were about hope, love, and the unbreakable spirit of people who refuse to be defined by their circumstances.

> **Lesson:** Carry the stories of those you meet as gifts, and let them shape how you live and connect with the world.

Redefining Purpose Through Travel

As I travelled, my sense of purpose evolved. It became less about personal ambition and more about making a difference—about finding ways to uplift others, even in small, everyday interactions. I realised that purpose isn't something grand or fixed; it's fluid, shaped by the lessons we gather and the connections we make.

In Kurdistan, I witnessed a Yazidi child being baptised—a moment of renewal and hope for a community that had endured so much. It was a reminder that purpose is often found in the quiet, everyday acts of faith and resilience. These moments showed me that purpose doesn't have to be monumental. It can be as simple as offering a kind word, sharing a meal, or listening to someone's story.

> **Lesson:** Purpose is not a destination; it's the sum of small, meaningful actions that leave the world a little better than we found it.

Leaving a Legacy of Kindness

The people I've met on my travels have taught me the importance of leaving behind a legacy—not of wealth or accomplishments, but of kindness and connection. They've shown me that the impact we have on others is the truest measure of a meaningful life.

In Iraq, the tailor's generosity reminded me that even in the face of loss, we have the power to choose how we respond to the world. In Lebanon, the hospitality of strangers taught me that connection transcends language, culture, and circumstance. These encounters have inspired me to live with intention, to prioritise relationships over achievements, and to focus on the small acts of kindness that ripple outward in ways we may never fully see.

> **Lesson:** Your legacy is defined not by what you achieve but by how you make others feel and the connections you leave behind.

The Journey Within

Ultimately, travel is not just a journey across borders; it's a journey within. It's about discovering who we are when the familiar is stripped away and we're left to navigate the unknown. Through travel, I've learned to embrace uncertainty, to trust in the unfolding of life, and to find meaning in every experience, no matter how small.

The roads I've walked, the people I've met, and the lessons I've learned have all led me to a deeper understanding of myself and the world. They've taught me that self-discovery is not a destination but an ongoing process—one that requires openness, curiosity, and a willingness to grow.

> **Lesson:** Self-discovery is a lifelong journey, and travel is one of its most powerful tools.

Travel has transformed the way I see myself and the world. It has taught me resilience, empathy, and the value of connection. It has shown me that purpose is not about achieving a grand vision but about living with intention, embracing uncertainty, and leaving a positive mark on those we encounter.

If there's one thing I've learned, it's that the journey is as important as the destination. Each step we take, each person we meet, and each lesson we learn adds to the tapestry of our lives. And through this tapestry, we find meaning—not in perfection, but in the beautiful, imperfect process of growth and connection.

For anyone seeking self-discovery, I would say this: Let travel be your teacher. Embrace the unfamiliar, seek out meaningful connections, and allow the world to challenge and change you. In doing so, you'll not only discover the world's beauty but also your own extraordinary potential.

> **Final Lesson:** Travel isn't just about exploring the world; it's about uncovering the depths of who we are and the heights of what we can become.

Advice for Finding Purpose Through Travel

Reflecting on my journeys and the lessons they've taught me, I've come to realise that travel is far more than a physical journey from one place to another—it's a path of discovery, growth, and connection. For those who seek to find purpose through travel, the journey begins with intention and openness. Here are some insights to guide you on your way:

1. Travel with Intention

Purposeful travel is not about ticking destinations off a list or capturing perfect photos for social media. It's about immersing yourself in the experience of a place—its culture, history, and people. This kind of travel demands curiosity and a willingness to go beyond the obvious.

Approach each new destination with the desire to learn and

connect. Before you set off, take time to understand the cultural, social, and historical context of the place you're visiting. Once there, step away from the tourist hotspots and seek authentic experiences. Visit local markets, talk to shopkeepers, and eat where the locals eat.

When I travelled through the Middle East, I didn't just admire the architecture or revel in the beauty of ancient ruins. I listened to stories from people who had lived through war, hardship, and displacement. Their resilience taught me lessons no guidebook ever could. They showed me that every place is more than its physical landmarks; it is a mosaic of human stories.

> **Takeaway:** Be intentional about why you're travelling. Ask yourself what you hope to learn or experience, and let that guide your journey.

2. Embrace Vulnerability

Travel has a way of humbling us. It places us in unfamiliar environments where we may not speak the language, understand the customs, or even know how to navigate the streets. These moments of vulnerability can be intimidating, but they are also opportunities for growth.

When you let yourself be vulnerable, you open the door to deeper connections and unexpected lessons. On my first trip to Nigeria as a child, I remember feeling overwhelmed by the sensory overload—the bustling markets, the cacophony of voices, the unfamiliar smells and sights. But as I allowed myself to embrace the chaos, I began to see the beauty within it. I watched children laughing and playing with makeshift toys, and I realised that joy doesn't depend on material wealth or perfect circumstances.

In Lebanon, when my wife and I were briefly detained due to a misunderstanding, I learned the importance of staying calm and open even in the face of fear. It was a vulnerable experience, but it taught me resilience and reminded me of the humanity that exists even in difficult situations.

> **Takeaway:** Let travel push you out of your comfort zone. Vulnerability is not weakness; it's a sign of openness and courage.

3. Find Meaning in the Small Moments

We often think of purpose as something grand—an epiphany, a life-changing event, or a transformative journey. But more often than not, purpose reveals itself in the small, seemingly ordinary moments.

During my travels, I've learned to pay attention to these moments. A shared laugh with a stranger, a kind gesture from someone who has little to give, or the quiet stillness of watching a sunset in an unfamiliar land—these experiences remind me of the beauty and interconnectedness of life.

In Syria, amidst the destruction left by years of conflict, I found meaning in the resilience of the people who welcomed us into their homes and shared stories of hope. In Iraq, a tailor who had lost everything still found it within himself to offer us food and drink, his generosity a powerful reminder that purpose can be as simple as making someone feel seen and valued.

> **Takeaway:** Look for purpose in the small, everyday moments. They are the threads that weave together a life of meaning.

4. Seek Connection Over Comfort

Travel has a way of stripping away our usual comforts, leaving us exposed to the raw realities of the world. In these moments, we have a choice: to retreat into ourselves or to reach out and connect with others.

In the Middle East, I saw how people living in uncertain and often dire circumstances relied on one another for strength and support. In Lebanon, I witnessed communities coming together to rebuild after conflict. In Kurdistan, I was moved by the Yazidi people's resilience as they held on to their traditions despite the horrors they had faced.

These experiences taught me that comfort is fleeting, but connection is lasting. Choosing connection means being present, listening with empathy, and allowing yourself to be changed by the people you meet.

> **Takeaway:** When you travel, prioritise relationships over convenience. The connections you make will outlast any material comfort.

5. Reflect on Your Experiences

It's easy to rush from one destination to the next, chasing new experiences without pausing to process what you've learned. But purposeful travel requires reflection. It's in the act of looking back that we find clarity, understanding, and growth.

After my journey through the Middle East, I took time to journal about my experiences—what I had seen, how I had felt, and what I had learned. This reflection helped me understand how those moments had shaped my sense of purpose. It allowed me to connect the dots between seemingly unrelated events and recognise the lessons that had emerged.

Reflection doesn't have to be complicated. It can be as simple as asking yourself a few questions at the end of each day: What surprised me today? What challenged me? What am I grateful for?

> **Takeaway:** Don't just experience; reflect. Purpose emerges when we take the time to understand the meaning behind our journeys.

The intersection of travel and purpose is not a single destination; it's an ongoing journey. Each place I visit, each person I meet, adds another layer to my understanding of what it means to live a meaningful life.

In Nigeria, I learned about resilience in the face of scarcity. In India, I saw how spirituality can provide solace and strength. In the Middle East, I witnessed humanity's capacity for both profound kindness and unyielding strength amidst hardship. Each of these lessons has shaped who I am and how I see the world.

Purpose, I've come to realise, is not a static goal—it's fluid and evolving. It's shaped by the lessons we gather along the way and the ways we choose to respond to those lessons. It's not something we "find" once and hold on to; it's something we build, moment by moment, encounter by encounter.

> **Takeaway:** Purpose is not fixed; it grows and changes with each experience. Embrace this fluidity as part of your journey.

The stories of the people I've met are my compass, guiding me towards a life rooted in empathy, resilience, and a desire to make a difference. They remind me that the world is vast, complex, and interconnected—and that our individual actions, no matter how small, have the power to create ripples of change.

The tailor in Mosul, the Yazidi child in Kurdistan, the man in Lebanon who offered us water despite the tense circumstances—these are the people who have left an indelible mark on my heart. Their stories are not just memories; they are lessons that I carry with me, shaping how I live, work, and connect with others.

> **Takeaway:** Let the stories you encounter guide you. They are not just moments in time; they are tools for growth and connection.

As I continue to travel, I think often about the legacy I want to leave behind. For me, it's not about wealth or accolades—it's about the impact I have on the people I meet. I want to leave a legacy of kindness, understanding, and connection, qualities that transcend borders, cultures, and time.

In every interaction, I try to embody the values I've learned through travel: empathy, resilience, and a commitment to living with purpose. Whether it's through my work, my relationships, or my personal adventures, I strive to make a positive difference in the lives of others.

> **Takeaway:** Your legacy is not defined by your achievements but by the lives you touch. Choose to leave a trail of kindness and connection.

Travel has taught me that purpose is not something we stumble upon; it's something we create through intention, vulnerability, connection, and reflection. It's a journey that never truly ends, but one that becomes richer with each step.

If there's one message I hope to leave with you, it's this: Purpose is not out there waiting to be found. It's within you, waiting to be uncovered through the experiences you embrace and the lessons you learn.

Let travel be your teacher, your guide, and your mirror. Allow it to challenge you, inspire you, and transform you. And as you journey through the world, remember that the greatest discoveries often lie not in the places you visit but in the person you become along the way.

Chapter 22

RESILIENCE, IMPACT, AND LOOKING FORWARD

Life is a collection of experiences, some shaping us more profoundly than others. My journey through the Middle East was one such defining chapter—a series of encounters that altered my understanding of resilience, clarified my sense of purpose, and ignited a drive to make a meaningful impact. Yet, the lessons from that trip were not confined to those moments; they carried forward, influencing every aspect of my life as I navigated the transition from corporate security to entrepreneurship and embraced a life of intention.

The journey since hasn't been easy, nor has it always been clear. But it has been deeply fulfilling. With each day, I continue to learn, adapt, and strive to embody resilience, live with purpose, and leave a lasting, positive impact.

The Power and Practice of Resilience

Resilience is often understood as the ability to endure hardship, but I've come to see it as much more than that. True resilience is about how we respond to life's uncertainties—not just enduring challenges but transforming them into opportunities for growth. This lesson came into sharp focus during my travels and deepened in the years that followed.

In the corporate world, resilience often meant navigating difficult workplace dynamics, meeting relentless deadlines, or maintaining composure under pressure. While these experiences were valuable, they didn't prepare me for the raw, unfiltered challenges of starting from scratch. When I left the corporate world to build Orca Advisory, I stepped into the unknown without a clear roadmap or a guaranteed outcome. Every decision, every step forward, tested my resilience in ways I had never imagined.

But resilience is not just a reaction to adversity—it's a proactive mindset. It's about embracing uncertainty with curiosity and courage. During my time in the Middle East, I saw resilience embodied by people living amidst unimaginable hardship. In Syria, Iraq, and Lebanon, I met individuals who had lost homes, loved ones, and stability, yet they carried on with remarkable grace. Their resilience wasn't rooted in grand gestures; it thrived in the quiet, daily acts of survival—finding joy in shared meals, extending kindness to strangers, and holding on to hope despite overwhelming odds.

Their example inspired me to approach challenges with a similar mindset. As I began building my business, I focused on small, steady steps forward rather than becoming overwhelmed by the bigger picture. Whether it was developing a new service, nurturing client relationships, or navigating financial uncertainties, I drew strength from the knowledge that resilience often flourishes in simplicity.

Resilience also requires self-compassion—something I've had to learn and relearn. There were days when doubts crept in: Had I made the right decision leaving corporate stability behind? Was I equipped to sustain both myself and my family in this new venture? In those moments, I had to remind myself that setbacks were not failures but stepping stones. By giving myself permission to stumble, to learn from mistakes, and to keep going, I discovered an inner strength that I hadn't fully tapped into before.

> **Key Lesson:** Resilience is not about perfection or unshakable strength. It's about the willingness to show up, adapt, and keep moving forward, even when the path is unclear. It's about finding meaning in the journey itself, no matter how challenging it may be.

Purpose and the Pursuit of Impact

As resilience became the foundation of my journey, purpose emerged as its guiding light. In the corporate world, purpose often felt secondary to profit margins and performance metrics. It wasn't that the work lacked value, but the impact often felt diluted by competing priorities. My experiences in the Middle East, however, reshaped my understanding of purpose, shifting my focus from personal achievement to meaningful contribution.

The people I met on that journey embodied purpose in profound ways. I think often of the tailor in Mosul, a man who had endured unimaginable loss—his children and wife taken from him, his life upended by violence. Yet he chose kindness over bitterness, welcoming us into his shop, sharing his story, and offering us food and drink. His purpose wasn't dictated by external success or recognition; it came from an inner resolve to live with dignity and compassion despite everything he had endured.

This encounter became a touchstone for me as I built Orca Advisory. I realised that purpose isn't about grand, world-changing achievements; it's about the small, daily actions that align with our values and contribute to others. Through teaching, coaching, consulting, and public speaking, I've made it my mission to help others uncover their own sense of purpose. Whether guiding clients towards meaningful career paths or encouraging organisations to align their practices with sustainability goals, I measure success by the positive ripples I create in the lives of others.

Purpose is also deeply personal, evolving with each experience. When I first left the corporate world, I saw purpose as a lofty ideal, something to be pursued and attained. But over time, I've come to see it as an ongoing process—a commitment to live intentionally and to seek impact in every interaction. Whether it's a workshop that helps someone find clarity or a conversation that sparks a new idea, each moment of connection reinforces the sense of purpose that drives me.

> **Key Lesson:** Purpose is not a destination but a practice. It's found in the small, cumulative acts of service, kindness, and dedication that create a meaningful life. It's about aligning our actions with our values and finding joy in the impact we have on others.

Lessons in Adaptability and Flexibility

Building a life rooted in resilience and purpose has required adaptability—a skill I honed through travel and have relied on ever since. Life is rarely a straight path, and my journey has been full of unexpected twists. From the relative stability of the corporate world to the uncertainty of entrepreneurship, each transition has been a lesson in flexibility.

Adaptability, I've found, is about more than just adjusting to external changes. It's about embracing the evolution of our own identity and purpose. When I started Orca Advisory, I had a clear vision of what I wanted to achieve, but that vision has grown and shifted with each new experience. As I've encountered new challenges, discovered new passions, and learned new skills, I've had to let go of rigid expectations and remain open to possibilities I hadn't considered before.

One of the greatest gifts of adaptability is the ability to approach life with curiosity rather than fear. Instead of seeing obstacles as threats, I try to view them as opportunities to learn and grow. This mindset has been particularly important in my work with clients, where every interaction is a chance to explore new perspectives and co-create solutions. By staying flexible and open, I've been able to navigate uncertainty with a sense of freedom and possibility.

> **Key Lesson:** Adaptability is a cornerstone of resilience and purpose. It's about staying open to change, embracing uncertainty, and finding strength in our ability to evolve. Flexibility allows us to see challenges not as barriers but as opportunities for growth.

As I look to the future, I carry with me the lessons of resilience, purpose, and adaptability. I don't know exactly where this path will lead, but I've come to trust that the journey is valuable in and of itself. Each day is an opportunity to learn, to connect, and to leave a positive mark on the world.

Moving forward, my focus is on deepening my impact—both personally and professionally. I want to continue helping others uncover their own sense of purpose, to inspire resilience in the face of challenges, and to encourage adaptability in a world that is constantly changing. Whether through workshops, speaking engagements, or one-on-one coaching, my goal is to create spaces where people feel empowered to live authentically and intentionally.

For readers navigating their own uncertain paths, my advice is simple: embrace the journey. Life will never be free of challenges, but each obstacle is an invitation to grow, to deepen your understanding of yourself, and to reaffirm your commitment to your values. Cultivating resilience, finding purpose, and striving for impact are not linear pursuits—they are practices that evolve with time and experience. Trust that each step forward, no matter how small, brings you closer to the life you are meant to live.

> **Key Lesson:** The future is uncertain, but that uncertainty is where growth, discovery, and transformation happen. Embrace it with courage, curiosity, and an unwavering commitment to live with purpose.

Resilience, purpose, and impact are not abstract ideals; they are daily practices that shape the way we live and connect with the world. My journey—from the corporate world to entrepreneurship, from the Middle East to the present—has taught me that life's greatest challenges are also its greatest teachers. Each setback, each success, and each unexpected turn has been an opportunity to grow, to serve, and to live more authentically.

Looking back, I see how every experience—whether joyful or painful—has added depth and meaning to my life. Moving forward, I am committed to honouring these lessons by living with resilience, pursuing purpose, and striving to make a positive impact. And as I continue on this path, I am reminded that the journey itself is the greatest reward—a journey filled with connection, discovery, and the endless potential to grow into the best version of ourselves.

Conclusion

A JOURNEY TO AUTHENTIC PURPOSE

Reflecting on the chapters of my life—marked by travel, professional evolution, and personal transformation—I am struck by how deeply interconnected these experiences are. Each step I have taken, whether planned or spontaneous, whether born of confidence or doubt, has contributed to a larger narrative: one of self-discovery, resilience, and the conscious pursuit of living in alignment with my values.

This journey has not been linear, nor has it been without its struggles. Yet, the challenges have become as meaningful as the victories, each one shaping me and refining my sense of purpose. Life rarely provides a clear map, but in hindsight, the patterns become undeniable. From the dusty streets of Nigeria to the war-torn cities of the Middle East, from corporate boardrooms driven by metrics to the uncharted waters of entrepreneurship, every experience has been a lesson—a building block in the ever-evolving pursuit of an authentic life.

Chapter 23
THE POWER OF PERSPECTIVE

Travel has been the most transformative lens through which I have come to understand the world and my place in it. Moving across continents during my formative years instilled in me the realisation that life is not a single, fixed narrative. Instead, it is a kaleidoscope of stories, each one offering a unique perspective.

Growing up in Nigeria, I witnessed the stark contrasts of wealth and poverty, joy and hardship. The bustling markets, alive with colour and sound, were not just places of commerce but also of community and resilience. People came together in ways that transcended economic disparity, finding joy in the small rituals of daily life. These early experiences planted the seeds of curiosity that would grow into a lifelong love for exploration.

Each place I have visited since has added new dimensions to my worldview. In India, I discovered the profound power of spirituality interwoven into the rhythms of daily life. In America, I experienced the tension between individuality and community, grappling with the need to adapt while preserving my identity. And in Australia, I learned to embrace balance, finding that success does not have to come at the expense of well-being.

Yet, nowhere was the transformative power of perspective more profound than in the Middle East. The region challenged me in ways I could never have anticipated. In Lebanon, Syria, and Iraq, I met people who had endured unimaginable loss—homes destroyed, families torn apart, futures uncertain. Yet, what struck me most was their unyielding spirit. They radiated kindness and hope, embodying resilience in its purest form.

These encounters reshaped my understanding of purpose. I came to see that purpose is not about avoiding hardship but about finding meaning within it. The people I met taught me that even in the face of profound adversity, there is room for love, connection, and hope.

The Universality of Connection

One of the most humbling lessons I've learned through my travels is that, despite surface differences, our shared humanity runs far deeper. No matter where I've been, the desires for connection, security, love, and purpose remain universal.

In a small shop in Beirut, a man who had lived through decades of conflict welcomed me with tea and stories. His shop, filled with photographs of a life built and rebuilt, stood as a testament to perseverance. In Mosul, a tailor who had lost his family to war offered me food and conversation, extending kindness despite his own pain. These moments of generosity, often from those who had the least to give, left indelible marks on my heart.

These encounters taught me that purpose doesn't require grand gestures. It is found in the small, meaningful moments—the warmth of a stranger's smile, the shared laughter over a meal, the quiet exchange of stories across cultures. Purpose is about honouring these connections, recognising that each one adds depth and meaning to our lives.

A Professional Evolution

While travel was my portal to self-discovery, my professional journey provided the structure within which I wrestled with questions of purpose. For years, I thrived in the corporate world, achieving milestones and gaining valuable skills. Yet, as the years passed, I began to feel a growing dissonance between what I valued and what the corporate environment rewarded.

The systems I worked within often prioritised profits over people, metrics over meaning. I found myself asking: *Is this enough?* The turning point came when I faced a particularly demeaning professional encounter—one that underscored the misalignment between my values and the corporate culture around me.

Quitting my job in February 2024 was not an impulsive decision. It was the culmination of years of reflection and an unwavering desire to reclaim my purpose. Guided by my father's wisdom and supported by my wife's belief in me, I took a leap of faith into the unknown.

Building Orka Advisory

Stepping into the world of entrepreneurship, I founded Orka Advisory with a mission to inspire, uplift, and create impact. The name "Orka," a Swedish word meaning "the will to get things done," encapsulates the ethos of my work. Orka isn't just about doing—it's about doing with intention and integrity, cutting through the noise to focus on what truly matters.

With no roadmap or business plan, I built Orka on four pillars: teaching, consulting, coaching, and public speaking. These were the areas where I felt I could contribute most authentically. My goal was ambitious yet simple: to positively impact 20,000 people within my first year. By announcing this publicly, I held myself accountable—not to profits, but to the lives I hoped to touch.

The early months were both exhilarating and challenging. There were moments of doubt when the uncertainty of entrepreneurship felt overwhelming. But each success—no matter how small—reinforced my commitment to this path. The stories of transformation from clients and participants became my markers of success.

One client shared that our coaching sessions helped her overcome her fear of failure, enabling her to take a bold step in her career. Another wrote to me weeks after a workshop, describing how a single exercise had reignited his confidence and sense of purpose. These stories remind me that purpose is not about personal achievement but about the ripple effects of our actions on others.

Lessons for the Journey

Looking back, the lessons I've learned feel universal, applicable to anyone seeking a life of purpose and authenticity.

1. **Embrace Uncertainty**: Growth happens when we step outside our comfort zones. The unknown is not something to fear but a space where transformation begins.
2. **Seek Connection**: Purpose is found in the relationships we build and the lives we touch. Whether through a shared meal, a heartfelt conversation, or an act of kindness, connection gives life its meaning.
3. **Redefine Success**: Let go of societal definitions of success and create your own. Success is not about reaching a final destination but about living in alignment with your values and making an impact.
4. **Practise Resilience**: Resilience is not about never falling; it's about rising each time we do. It's about finding strength in vulnerability and choosing to keep moving forward, no matter the obstacles.

5. **Live with Intention**: Purpose is not a destination; it's a practice. Each day is an opportunity to live with integrity, to align your actions with your values, and to make a positive difference.

The journey ahead remains uncertain, but that is where its beauty lies. Each new day, each new encounter, is an opportunity to grow, to connect, and to make a difference. Orka Advisory is still in its early stages, but it is a reflection of everything I value—purpose, resilience, and connection.

My hope is that through Orka, I can continue to inspire others to embrace their own journeys, to step into the unknown with courage, and to live lives of intention and authenticity. The work I do now is not just about helping people achieve their professional goals; it's about helping them align their lives with their values and discover the deeper sense of purpose that comes from making an impact.

For those reading this, I hope my story serves as an invitation to reflect on your own journey. Purpose is not something we find—it is something we create. It is built moment by moment, through the choices we make and the connections we nurture.

You don't need to have all the answers. Start with what feels true to you. Take the first step, even if it's small, and trust that the journey will reveal itself as you go. Purpose is not about perfection; it's about persistence, about showing up for yourself and others with courage and authenticity.

As I continue on this path, I am reminded every day that purpose is not a destination; it is a way of being. It is about living with resilience, embracing the unknown, and remaining committed to making the world a little better than we found it.

And that, I believe, is the true essence of a journey to authentic purpose.

Chapter 24

FROM STAGNATION TO FREEDOM

For nearly two decades, the corporate world defined my professional identity. It was a realm of structure, opportunity, and growth—a place where I could test my skills, broaden my knowledge, and build a career. Yet, as the years passed, I found myself increasingly disillusioned. While I valued the lessons and achievements that the corporate world had brought me, I couldn't ignore its inherent flaws. Too often, the systems prioritised profits over people, metrics over meaning, and superficial accomplishments over genuine impact.

Despite achieving what many would call professional "success," I found myself asking a fundamental question: *Is this enough?*

A Moment of Reckoning

The breaking point came in August 2023 during a particularly challenging professional encounter. That morning, I had done a dry run of a strategy presentation with my manager. His critique wasn't openly hostile, but it was steeped in condescension—a dismissal not only of my work but of my character. It was the kind of feedback that chips away at one's confidence, delivered in a manner that was needlessly harsh. Hours later, I presented the same strategy to the board, and they unanimously endorsed it.

The validation from the board should have felt like a triumph, but instead, it left me with a bitter taste. The dissonance between what I valued—respect, collaboration, authenticity—and what the corporate world often rewarded became glaringly clear. I realised that the systems I had worked so hard to navigate no longer aligned with who I was or who I wanted to be.

That evening, I called my father. He was in India, unwell but as wise and perceptive as ever. I laid it all out, asking him a question that had been haunting me: "Is it just me? Am I too nice, too soft? Am I the problem?"

He paused for a moment before responding: "It's not you, but it is you. You're not the root of the problem, but you are the one with the power to change it. You have the skills and the knowledge to make an impact—don't waste that by staying with people who don't align with your values."

His words were a call to action. They resonated deeply, affirming what I already knew in my heart: I had outgrown this path. Staying in the corporate world any longer would mean compromising my integrity, my values, and my potential.

Taking the Leap

Returning to Melbourne, I turned to my "circle of trust"—a close-knit group of friends, mentors, and confidants—and asked them what I should do next. Their advice was nearly unanimous: It was time to forge a new path.

Yet, the decision wasn't mine alone to make. I approached my wife with the same question, fully aware of the risks involved. "If I can make enough to keep food on the table, pay the bills, and allow us to travel once or twice a year, would that be enough?"

She hesitated at first, her concerns understandable. We were a single-income household, and this leap of faith would mean trading the stability of a steady paycheck for the uncertainty of entrepreneurship. But her belief in me ultimately won out. "If this is what you need to do," she said, "then I'll support you."

Her support became the foundation on which I built this new chapter. My mother, too, was a steadfast believer in my potential. She had always encouraged me to dream big and take bold steps, even when the odds seemed daunting. Her unwavering faith reminded me that while the journey ahead would be uncertain, it was also filled with possibility.

And so, in February 2024, I quit.

The Freedom to Redefine Success

Quitting my job wasn't just about leaving the corporate world; it was about reclaiming my sense of purpose. For years, I had measured success by external metrics—titles, bonuses, accolades—but now, I wanted something different. I wanted a life and career defined by meaning, integrity, and impact.

The first few weeks were a whirlwind of emotions: excitement, doubt, fear, and relief. There was no roadmap, no predefined plan. For the first time in years, I was entirely responsible for charting my own course.

I began by reflecting on the things I truly loved—teaching, coaching, consulting, and public speaking—and considering how I could build a business around these passions. Slowly, the pieces started to come together. I envisioned a venture rooted in four core pillars, one that would allow me to help others become the best versions of themselves while staying true to my own values.

Orka Advisory: A New Beginning

As I mulled over a name for this new venture, I wanted something that encapsulated my ethos—a commitment to action, resilience, and authenticity. My search led me to "Orka," a Swedish word that translates to "the will to get things done." It was perfect.

Orka Advisory was born, not from a carefully crafted business plan but from a deep sense of purpose. My mission was simple yet ambitious: to positively impact 20,000 people within my first year. I publicly announced this goal, holding myself accountable not to profits or performance metrics but to the lives I hoped to touch.

Building Orka was both exhilarating and challenging. There were moments of doubt when I questioned whether I had made the right decision, moments when the financial uncertainty felt overwhelming. But even in those moments, I reminded myself why I had chosen this path.

Lessons from the Middle East

My travels through the Middle East played a significant role in reinforcing my commitment to this journey. In Lebanon, Syria, and Iraq, I had met people who exemplified resilience in the face of unimaginable adversity. They had lost homes, loved ones, and a sense of security, yet they continued to rebuild their lives with courage and grace.

These encounters taught me that purpose isn't about avoiding hardship; it's about finding meaning in the face of it. The people I met did not define themselves by their losses but by their ability to rise above them. Their resilience became a source of inspiration for me, reminding me that the challenges I faced were small in comparison.

The Middle East also taught me the importance of community. In places where resources were scarce and uncertainty was high, people relied on one another in ways that were deeply moving. This sense of connection became a guiding principle for me as I built Orka. I wanted my work to be about more than just individual success; I wanted it to contribute to a larger collective, to foster a world where compassion and collaboration are the norm.

Redefining Success

One of the most liberating aspects of this journey has been redefining what success means to me. In the corporate world, success often felt like a moving target, tied to external validation and performance metrics. At Orka, success is measured not in numbers but in stories, in moments of transformation, and in the lives I am privileged to touch.

This shift in perspective has allowed me to approach my work with a sense of freedom and authenticity. I no longer feel constrained by the need to prove myself or to meet someone else's definition of achievement. Instead, I focus on staying true to my values and doing work that feels meaningful.

Success, I've learned, is not about reaching a final destination but about the journey itself. It's about showing up each day with intention, doing work that aligns with your values, and making a positive impact on the world around you.

The Ripple Effect

Every interaction at Orka, no matter how small, has the potential to create a ripple effect. Whether it's helping an executive align their leadership style with their values, guiding a young professional towards a career that feels authentic, or inspiring a room full of people during a speaking engagement, each moment of connection has the power to create lasting impact.

One of the most rewarding aspects of this journey has been

hearing the stories of transformation from those I've worked with. A client once shared that our coaching sessions helped her overcome a paralysing fear of failure, allowing her to take a leap of faith in her career. Another participant in a workshop wrote to me weeks later, describing how a simple exercise we had done helped him rebuild his confidence and approach his work with renewed energy.

These stories are a testament to the power of intention and the importance of meeting people where they are. They reinforce my belief that purpose is not about grand gestures or sweeping changes; it's about showing up, listening, and making a difference in the lives of others, one interaction at a time.

As I look to the future, I am filled with a sense of possibility. Orka Advisory is still in its early stages, and there is so much more I hope to accomplish. But even as I set new goals and envision new opportunities, I remain grounded in the purpose that brought me here.

The journey ahead will undoubtedly bring its own set of challenges, but I am ready to face them with the same resilience, adaptability, and intention that have guided me thus far. I am excited to continue growing Orka, to expand its reach, and to deepen its impact.

More importantly, I am committed to staying true to the values that have shaped this journey. I want Orka to be a reflection not just of what I do but of who I am—a reminder that purpose is not about perfection but about persistence, that success is not about accumulation but about contribution.

For those reading this, I hope my story serves as an invitation to reflect on your own journey. Whether you are navigating a career transition, seeking a deeper sense of purpose, or simply trying to make sense of life's complexities, I encourage you to take that first step.

Purpose is not something we find; it is something we create. It is built moment by moment, through the choices we make and the lives we touch. It is not about having all the answers but about being willing to ask the right questions and to embrace the journey, however uncertain it may be.

As I continue on this path, I am reminded every day that purpose is not a destination; it is a way of being. It is about living with intention, with resilience, and with a commitment to making the world a little better than we found it.

And that, I believe, is the true essence of moving from stagnation to freedom.

Chapter 25
PURPOSE BEYOND PROFIT

Stepping into the unknown, I founded Orka Advisory with a clear mission: to inspire, uplift, and create meaningful impact. The name "Orka," a Swedish word meaning "the will to get things done," perfectly encapsulated my ethos. It symbolised more than just action; it embodied a purposeful drive to focus on what truly matters and to make every effort count. It was a reflection of the journey that brought me here, shaped by my experiences in the corporate world, my travels across the Middle East, and the courage to chart an uncharted course.

The first months after leaving my corporate career were both exhilarating and intimidating. On one hand, I was free—free to design a life aligned with my values, free to prioritise purpose over profit. On the other hand, I faced the daunting challenge of building something from the ground up with no guarantees of success. There was no roadmap, no predetermined business model. I had to rely on my instincts, my passions, and the lessons I had learned through years of professional and personal exploration.

From the outset, Orka Advisory was built on four core pillars: teaching, consulting, coaching, and public speaking. These were not just services I could offer; they were expressions of the ways I could contribute most authentically to others. I had spent years refining my skills in these areas, but it was no longer about fulfilling a corporate mandate or achieving quarterly targets. It was about creating real change—helping individuals and organisations align their actions with their values and inspiring them to live and work with intention.

My mission was ambitious: to positively impact 20,000 people within my first year. It was more than a goal; it was a commitment to myself and to the people I aimed to serve. By announcing this goal publicly, I held myself accountable—not to profits or metrics, but to the lives I hoped to touch. It was a bold step, but one that felt deeply aligned with the purpose I was pursuing.

The journey of building Orka Advisory has been one of constant learning and adaptation. Without a rigid business plan or marketing strategy, I approached each day as an opportunity to experiment, to listen, and to refine. This flexibility allowed me to stay open to new ideas and to tailor my offerings to the needs of those I worked with.

For example, in my teaching engagements, I quickly realised that people were not just looking for expertise—they were looking for connection, inspiration, and a sense of possibility. Similarly, in my coaching sessions, I learned that the most profound transformations often came not from providing answers but from asking the right questions. Each interaction taught me something new, and with every step, Orka began to take on a life of its own, shaped by the people I served.

The challenges of entrepreneurship were not limited to professional hurdles; they also demanded a great deal of personal resilience. There were days of doubt, moments of financial uncertainty, and times when I wondered whether I had made the right decision in leaving the corporate world. But each time I faced these challenges, I drew strength from the purpose that had brought me here.

One of the most important lessons I've learned through Orka is that purpose is not a destination; it is a journey. It evolves as we grow, as we meet new people, and as we navigate life's twists and turns. When I first set out to create Orka, my purpose was clear but still somewhat abstract. I wanted to inspire others and make a difference. But over time, this purpose became more tangible, shaped by the stories of those I worked with and the impact we were able to create together.

Success, which I had once measured by titles, promotions, and accolades, now felt more meaningful when I received an email from a client who had gained clarity on their life's direction, or when a participant in one of my workshops shared how a single insight had changed their perspective. These moments reminded me that purpose is not about what we achieve for ourselves; it is about the ripple effects of our actions on others.

Every interaction at Orka, no matter how small, has the potential to create a ripple effect. Whether it's helping an executive align their leadership style with their values, guiding a young professional towards a career that feels authentic, or inspiring a room full of people during a speaking engagement, each moment of connection has the power to create lasting impact.

My travels through the Middle East continue to inform and inspire the work I do at Orka. The resilience I witnessed in people who had faced unimaginable hardship serves as a constant reminder of the strength that lies within all of us. In Lebanon, Syria, and Iraq, I met individuals who had lost their homes, their loved ones, and their sense of security, yet they continued to rebuild their lives with courage and grace.

These encounters taught me that purpose is not about avoiding hardship but about finding meaning in the face of it. The people I met did not define themselves by their losses but by their ability to rise above them. This resilience, this determination to create beauty and connection amidst adversity, is what I strive to emulate in my own life and work.

The Middle East also reinforced the importance of community. In places where resources were scarce and uncertainty was high, people relied on one another in ways that were deeply inspiring. This sense of connection—of shared humanity—has become a guiding principle for me. It reminds me that the work I do at Orka is not just about individual success; it is about contributing to a larger collective, about building a world where compassion and collaboration are the norm.

One of the most liberating aspects of this journey has been redefining what success means to me. In the corporate world, success often felt like a moving target, tied to external validation and performance metrics. At Orka, success is measured not in numbers but in stories, in moments of transformation, and in the lives I am privileged to touch.

This shift in perspective has allowed me to approach my work with a sense of freedom and authenticity. I no longer feel constrained by the need to prove myself or to meet someone else's definition of achievement. Instead, I focus on staying true to my values and doing work that feels meaningful.

Success, I've learned, is not about reaching a final destination but about the journey itself. It's about showing up each day with intention, doing work that aligns with your values, and making a positive impact on the world around you.

As I look to the future, I am filled with a sense of possibility. Orka Advisory is still in its early stages, and there is so much more I hope to accomplish. But even as I set new goals and envision new opportunities, I remain grounded in the purpose that brought me here.

The journey ahead will undoubtedly bring its own set of challenges, but I am ready to face them with the same resilience, adaptability, and intention that have guided me thus far. I am excited to continue growing Orka, to expand its reach, and to deepen its impact.

More importantly, I am committed to staying true to the values that have shaped this journey. I want Orka to be a reflection not just of what I do but of who I am—a reminder that purpose is not about perfection but about persistence, that success is not about accumulation but about contribution.

For those reading this, I hope my story serves as an invitation to reflect on your own journey. Whether you are navigating a career transition, seeking a deeper sense of purpose, or simply trying to make sense of life's complexities, I encourage you to take that first step.

Purpose is not something we find; it is something we create. It is built moment by moment, through the choices we make and the lives we touch. It is not about having all the answers but about being willing to ask the right questions and to embrace the journey, however uncertain it may be.

As I continue on this path, I am reminded every day that purpose is not a destination; it is a way of being. It is about living with intention, with resilience, and with a commitment to making the world a little better than we found it.

And that, I believe, is the true essence of purpose beyond profit.

Chapter 26
THE PRACTICE OF RESILIENCE

Resilience has been a constant theme throughout my journey. Whether navigating the uncertainty of new cultures, enduring setbacks in the corporate world, or building a business from scratch, resilience has been my anchor. But I've come to understand that resilience is not about simply enduring—it's about adapting, learning, and finding strength in vulnerability.

The people I met during my travels exemplified resilience in its purest form. In Mosul, the tailor who had lost everything yet continued to offer kindness to strangers taught me that resilience is an act of defiance—a refusal to let circumstances define you. His story inspired me to approach my own challenges with the same quiet strength and unwavering purpose.

In my professional life, resilience has meant embracing uncertainty and letting go of the need for control. It has meant forgiving myself for mistakes and allowing room for growth. Resilience, I've learned, is not a solitary practice; it is cultivated through connection, support, and the belief that even in the face of setbacks, we have the power to move forward.

As I reflect on the milestones, challenges, and revelations that have shaped my life, I am struck by the universality of the lessons I've learned. These truths transcend individual circumstances and resonate with anyone striving to live a purposeful and authentic life. While my journey has been uniquely mine—filled with travel, pivotal decisions, and moments of vulnerability—the insights I've gained are ones I believe we all can embrace.

Here are five guiding principles for the journey ahead, drawn from the twists and turns of my life, and offered as a compass for those navigating their own paths towards meaning and fulfillment.

1. Embrace Uncertainty

Growth happens in the spaces where we feel most unsure of ourselves. The unknown, far from being a place of fear, is fertile ground for transformation. This lesson has been a recurring theme in my life, from my corporate career to the adventures that took me across the Middle East.

I think back to the moment I decided to quit my job—a leap into uncertainty with no safety net. For years, I had followed a traditional path, one that promised stability but left me feeling unfulfilled. Walking away from the corporate world meant relinquishing that stability, stepping into a world of unknowns. I had no business plan, no guarantees, only a vision of a life where my work aligned with my values.

In hindsight, it's clear that uncertainty was not my enemy—it was my greatest ally. It forced me to examine my motivations, adapt to new challenges, and trust in my ability to navigate unfamiliar territory. The discomfort of not knowing was, in many ways, the crucible where my purpose was forged.

My travels also taught me to embrace the unknown. Whether crossing into Syria amidst visible scars of conflict or sitting in a small café in Baghdad listening to stories of resilience, I found myself stepping far outside my comfort zone. In these moments, I discovered a deeper connection to humanity and a greater sense of my own capacity for growth.

Uncertainty, I've come to realise, is not a void to be avoided but a space where life's most meaningful experiences occur. It is in the unpredictability of life that we find our strength, our courage, and our purpose.

2. Seek Connection

At the heart of every meaningful experience in my life has been connection. The relationships we build, the lives we touch, and the shared moments of humanity are what truly give life its richness.

One of the most profound connections I've experienced was with a tailor in Mosul, Iraq. This man, who had lost his family to war, welcomed me into his shop with warmth and generosity that belied the immense pain he had endured. He shared his story, offered me food, and reminded me that even amidst profound loss, kindness can flourish.

Moments like these have reinforced a central truth: purpose is not about individual achievement but about the bonds we form with others. Whether it's the kindness of a stranger or the support of loved ones, connection is the thread that weaves meaning into our lives.

Building Orka Advisory has allowed me to deepen this understanding. Each coaching session, workshop, and speaking engagement is an opportunity to connect with others on their own journeys. Seeing someone gain clarity, rediscover their passions, or overcome a challenge fills me with a sense of fulfillment that no material achievement could match.

The lesson is simple but profound: seek connection over convenience, relationships over results, and shared humanity over personal gain. In the end, it is the people we meet and the lives we touch that leave the most lasting impact.

3. Redefine Success

For much of my life, I pursued success as society defines it—titles, accolades, and financial stability. But over time, I began to question whether this version of success aligned with who I was and what I valued.

The turning point came during my travels through the Middle East. Witnessing the resilience and grace of people living amidst war and hardship forced me to reconsider what it means to lead a successful life. In Aleppo, I met families who had lost everything yet continued to rebuild with hope and determination. In Lebanon, a shopkeeper who had endured years of instability still greeted every customer with warmth and generosity. Their lives, though marked by struggle, were defined by a deeper kind of success—a success rooted in courage, compassion, and community.

Leaving the corporate world was my way of redefining success on my own terms. For me, success is no longer about external validation; it's about living in alignment with my values and making a positive impact. Through Orka Advisory, I measure success not in profits but in the lives I touch and the change I inspire.

This shift has been liberating. It has allowed me to focus on what truly matters—connection, growth, and purpose. I encourage others to let go of societal expectations and create their own definitions of success. True success is not a final destination but a journey of living authentically and intentionally.

4. Practise Resilience

Resilience is often misunderstood as an innate quality, something we either have or don't. But I've learned that resilience is a practice, a skill we cultivate through experience, reflection, and choice. It is not about never falling but about rising each time we do.

My travels through conflict zones were a masterclass in resilience. In Syria, I met people who had rebuilt their lives multiple times, each time with unwavering determination. In Iraq, I saw communities coming together to heal after years of devastation. And in Lebanon, I experienced resilience firsthand when my wife and I were taken hostage by Hezbollah.

That experience tested every ounce of my strength, both physical and emotional. Yet, even in those tense hours, I witnessed acts of humanity that reminded me of the resilience inherent in all of us. A kind word from one of our captors, a shared meal, and the eventual resolution of the ordeal—all of these moments underscored the power of resilience to transcend even the most challenging circumstances.

In my own life, resilience has meant embracing setbacks as opportunities for growth. Leaving the corporate world to start Orka Advisory was not without its challenges. There were moments of doubt, financial uncertainty, and fear of failure. But each time I faced these obstacles, I chose to keep moving forward, drawing strength from the lessons I'd learned along the way.

Resilience is not about avoiding hardship; it's about meeting it head-on, learning from it, and using it as a foundation for growth.

5. Live with Intention

Purpose is not a destination; it's a practice. It is something we cultivate daily through our actions, decisions, and interactions. Living with intention means aligning your choices with your values and approaching each day as an opportunity to make a difference.

Starting Orka Advisory was an exercise in intentional living. I wanted to create a venture that reflected my values, my passions, and my commitment to making a positive impact. Every decision, from the name "Orka" to the focus on teaching, coaching, and consulting, was made with purpose.

Living with intention has also meant prioritising what matters most. It's about being present in the moment, valuing quality over quantity, and making time for the people and activities that bring joy and fulfillment. It's about saying no to what doesn't serve you so that you can say yes to what does.

This lesson has been especially meaningful in my personal life. My wife's unwavering support during my transition from the corporate world reminded me of the importance of aligning my personal and professional lives with my values. Together, we've built a life that prioritises connection, authenticity, and shared purpose.

As I reflect on these lessons, I am filled with gratitude for the journey that has brought me here. Each experience, whether joyful or painful, has shaped me in profound ways. The lessons of embracing uncertainty, seeking connection, redefining success, practising resilience, and living with intention are not just guideposts for the past; they are principles I carry with me as I look to the future.

The journey is far from over, and that is what excites me most. Each new day is an opportunity to learn, grow, and make an impact. My hope is that these lessons resonate with others, inspiring them to embark on their own journeys of purpose and authenticity.

Life is not a straight path, but within its twists and turns lies the potential for transformation. By embracing the unknown, connecting with others, and living with intention, we can create lives that are not only meaningful but also deeply fulfilling.

In the end, it's not about where we end up but how we live along the way. And that, I believe, is the greatest lesson of all.

Chapter 27
A LIFE OF PURPOSE

Life rarely unfolds as we imagine it. The journey to understanding who we are and what we value is rarely a straight path. It's filled with moments of clarity and confusion, of triumph and setback. Yet, it is precisely these twists and turns that give life its meaning. My journey—spanning continents, corporate boardrooms, conflict zones, and personal transformation—has been anything but linear. But it's within this nonlinear path that I've found purpose, built moment by moment through the choices I've made and the lives I've been privileged to touch.

Purpose, I've learned, is not something that suddenly appears fully formed. It's not a revelation that strikes like lightning, but a slow, deliberate process of uncovering. My journey began with an early fascination for travel, a curiosity about the world that grew into a lifelong passion for exploration. Travel taught me early on that life is not confined to the routines or expectations we inherit; it is a vast landscape of experiences waiting to be discovered.

Through my time in the Middle East, I came face-to-face with both beauty and hardship. I met people whose resilience in the face of unimaginable adversity humbled and inspired me. Their courage to carry on amidst loss and devastation forced me to reflect on my own life and the choices I had made. These encounters illuminated a profound truth: purpose isn't about avoiding challenges; it's about embracing them and allowing them to shape us into better versions of ourselves.

In Lebanon, my wife and I faced one of the most harrowing experiences of our lives. Being taken hostage by Hezbollah was a moment that could have broken me, but instead, it became a crucible for transformation. In the hours we were detained, I experienced fear, vulnerability, and helplessness like never before. Yet, even in those dark moments, there were flashes of humanity—kindness from a guard, reassurance that we would be released. These small acts reminded me that even in the most challenging circumstances, there is space for compassion and connection.

When we were finally released, the relief was overwhelming, but so was the clarity that followed. That experience crystallised my understanding of resilience—not just as the ability to endure hardship, but as the willingness to find meaning in it. Life is fragile, unpredictable, and often unfair. Yet, within that fragility lies the opportunity to choose how we respond, to build strength from struggle, and to turn our pain into purpose.

Returning home, the lessons from the Middle East began to intersect with my professional life. For two decades, I had climbed the corporate ladder, achieving success by conventional standards. I worked in industries that spanned consulting, healthcare, sustainability, and resources, garnering awards and accolades along the way. But beneath the surface, I felt increasingly disconnected. The corporate world, with its emphasis on profit over people and process over purpose, began to feel misaligned with my values.

The decision to leave wasn't easy. Walking away from a stable career meant stepping into the unknown. But stability is not the same as fulfillment. As I reflected on my experiences in the corporate world, I realised that I was holding on to something that no longer served me. The toxic behaviours I encountered, the lack of alignment with my personal values, and the yearning for something more meaningful became impossible to ignore.

I turned to my father for guidance, sharing my doubts and frustrations. His words cut through my uncertainty with startling clarity: "It's not you, but it is you. You know what you need to do. Don't waste your potential in places that don't align with who you are."

With his support, and that of my wife, I made the leap. In February 2024, I resigned from my corporate role. For the first time in my career, I had no plan B, no fallback position. But I carried with me a newfound sense of purpose and a deep belief in the possibility of building something aligned with my values.

As I pondered my next steps, I kept returning to the lessons I had learned on my travels. I thought about the tailor in Mosul who, despite losing his family, lived with dignity and kindness. I thought about the people of Aleppo and Beirut who rebuilt their lives amidst ruins. These individuals didn't let their circumstances define them; they chose to create meaning and purpose despite it all.

Inspired by these stories, I founded Orka Advisory. The name itself is derived from a Swedish word meaning "the will to get things done." It embodies resilience, action, and the commitment to make an impact. Orka Advisory was built on four pillars: teaching, coaching, consulting, and public speaking. Through these avenues, I sought to help individuals and organisations find alignment between their actions and values, to inspire them to lead with purpose and integrity.

My goal was ambitious but deeply personal: to positively impact 20,000 people in the first year. This wasn't a target set for accolades or marketing—it was a promise to myself to measure success not in profits but in lives touched.

Building Orka Advisory has been one of the most challenging yet fulfilling chapters of my life. Each day brings its own uncertainties, but it also brings freedom—the freedom to create, to lead, and to live authentically. For the first time, I feel that my work is a true reflection of who I am and what I stand for.

Through coaching sessions, workshops, and speaking engagements, I've witnessed the transformative power of purpose. I've seen clients rediscover their passions, align their careers with their values, and embrace their potential. Their journeys remind me why I took this leap of faith.

But this isn't just about helping others; it's about the ongoing process of my own growth. Every interaction teaches me something new, challenges me to be better, and reinforces my belief that purpose is not a destination but a way of being.

If there's one thing I've learned, it's that purpose is deeply personal. It doesn't look the same for everyone, and it doesn't follow a set timeline. But there are universal truths that have guided me on this journey:

- **Start with What Feels True:** Purpose begins with authenticity. It's not about conforming to societal expectations but about listening to your inner voice and honouring what feels right for you.
- **Embrace the Unknown:** Growth often requires stepping into discomfort. Whether it's leaving a secure job or travelling to a foreign land, the unknown holds the potential for transformation.
- **Focus on Connection:** Purpose is rarely found in isolation. It's in the relationships we build, the lives we touch, and the shared humanity we experience.

- **Find Meaning in Adversity:** Challenges are inevitable, but they are also opportunities to learn, grow, and redefine our priorities.

To anyone reading this who feels trapped by convention or unsure of their next step, I offer this encouragement: You don't need to have all the answers. Start with one step, no matter how small, and trust that the path will unfold. Purpose is not about perfection; it's about showing up with courage, persistence, and an open heart.

As I continue my journey, I carry with me the lessons of travel, the strength of resilience, and the guiding light of connection. Orka Advisory is more than a business—it's a reflection of my commitment to inspire, empower, and create impact. It's a reminder that our greatest potential lies not in what we achieve for ourselves, but in what we contribute to the world.

The journey is never complete, and that's what makes it beautiful. Each new day, each new encounter, is an opportunity to grow, to connect, and to make a difference. And in the end, that's what purpose is all about—a life lived fully, authentically, and with unwavering hope for what lies ahead.

Be Published

Publish through a successful publisher.
Brolga Publishing is represented through:
• National book trade distribution, including sales, marketing & distribution through Simon & Schuster.
• International book trade distribution to:
    - The United Kingdom
    - Sales representation in South East Asia
• Worldwide e-Book distribution

For details and enquiries, contact:
Brolga Publishing Pty Ltd
ABN 46 063 962 443
PO Box 452
Torquay Victoria 3228
Australia

markzocchi@brolgapublishing.com.au
(Email for a catalogue request)